The Majority Press

# THE POETICAL WORKS OF MARCUS GARVEY

TONY MARTIN established himself as the leading scholar of the Garvey Movement with his *Race First: The Ideological and Organizational Struggles of Marcus Garvey and the Universal Negro Improvement Association* (1976). He followed this up with *The Pan-African Connection* (1983). He also co-authored *Rare Afro-Americana: A Reconstruction of the Adger Library* (1981).

Martin is professor and chairman of the Black Studies Department at Wellesley College, Massachusetts. He did his M.A. and Ph.D. in history at Michigan State University and the B.Sc. in economics at the University of Hull, England. In 1965 he qualified as a barrister-at-law at Gray's Inn, London. He has taught at the University of Michigan-Flint, the Cipriani Labor College (Trinidad) and St. Mary's College (Trinidad). He has been visiting professor at the University of Minnesota and Brandeis University.

D1571742

# Books from The Majority Press, Inc.

## THE NEW MARCUS GARVEY LIBRARY

Literary Garveyism: Garvey, Black Arts and the Harlem Renaissance. Tony Martin. $19.95 (cloth), $9.95 (paper).

The Poetical Works of Marcus Garvey. Tony Martin, Ed. $17.95 (cloth), $9.95 (paper).

Marcus Garvey, Hero: A First Biography. Tony Martin. $9.95 (paper).

The Pan-African Connection. Tony Martin. $10.95 (paper).

Message to the People: The Course of African Philosophy. Marcus Garvey. Ed. by Tony Martin. $22.95 (cloth), $9.95 (paper).

Race First: The Ideological and Organizational Struggles of Marcus Garvey and the Universal Negro Improvement Association. Tony Martin. $12.95 (paper).

The Philosophy and Opinions of Marcus Garvey. Amy Jacques Garvey, Ed. $14.95 (paper).

Amy Ashwood Garvey: Pan-Africanist, Feminist and Wife No. 1. Tony Martin. Forthcoming.

African Fundamentalism: A Literary and Cultural Anthology of Garvey's Harlem Renaissance. Tony Martin, Ed. $14.95 (paper).

## THE BLACK WORLD

Brazil: Mixture or Massacre? Essays in the Genocide of a Black People. Abdias do Nascimento. $12.95 (paper).

Studies in the African Diaspora: A Memorial to James R. Hooker (1929-1976). John P. Henderson and Harry A. Reed, Eds. $39.95 (cloth).

In Nobody's Backyard: The Grenada Revolution in its Own Words. Vol. II, Facing the World. Tony Martin, Ed. $22.95 (cloth).

Guinea's Other Suns: The African Dynamic in Trinidad Culture. Maureen Warner-Lewis. $9.95 (paper).

Carlos Cooks: And Black Nationalism from Garvey to Malcolm. Robert, Nyota and Grandassa Harris, Eds. $9.95 (paper).

From Kingston to Kenya: The Making of a Pan-Africanist Lawyer. Dudley Thompson, with Margaret Cezair Thompson. $10.95 (paper).

The Jewish Onslaught: Despatches from the Wellesley Battlefront. Tony Martin. $9.95 (paper).

The Afro-Trinidadian: Endangered Species/Oh, What a Nation! Tony Martin. Forthcoming.

Marcus Garvey/Makis Gave. Florie-N Chevry-Saintil. $9.95 (paper). [In Haitian Creole].

Eyes to My Soul: The Rise or Decline of a Black FBI Agent. Tyrone Powers. $14.95.

*Order from The Majority Press, Inc., P.O. Box 538, Dover, MA 02030, U.S.A. Mass. residents add 5% sales tax.*

# THE POETICAL WORKS OF MARCUS GARVEY

## Edited by
## TONY MARTIN

*The New Marcus Garvey Library, No. 2*

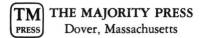

**THE MAJORITY PRESS**
Dover, Massachusetts

Library of Congress Cataloging in Publication Data

Garvey, Marcus, 1887-1940.
    The poetical works of Marcus Garvey.

    (The New Marcus Garvey library; no. 2)
    Bibliography: p.
    I. Martin, Tony, 1942-      . II. Title.
III. Series: Martin, Tony, 1942-        . New Marcus
Garvey library; no. 2.
PS3513.A7417A17        1983        811'.52        83-61114
ISBN 0-912469-02-1
ISBN 0-912469-03-X (pbk.)

First published in 1983, simultaneously in hardbound and paperback volumes.

The Majority Press
P.O. Box 538
Dover, Massachusetts 02030

Printed in the United States of America

    9 8 7 6 5

# Contents

Preface                                                              ix

1   *The Tragedy of White Injustice* (1927)                          1

2   *Selections from the Poetic Meditations
    of Marcus Garvey* (1927)                                        27

3   "Keep Cool" (1927)                                              53

4   From the *Negro World* (1927)                                   57

5   From the *Black Man* (1933-1939)                                63

6   From *Universal Negro Improvement
    Association Convention Hymns*
    (1934)                                                         109

    Bibliographical Note                                           121

# Preface

Marcus Garvey was many things—race leader, journalist, orator and ideologist, to name a few. He was also a poet, and his poetical works are collected here for the first time. They appeared originally in pamphlet form and in some of his own publications. His followers were fond of them and often recited them at concerts and political meetings. Veteran Garvey-ites can still be found who have not forgotten the verses they committed to memory many decades ago.

To say that Garvey's poetry was without significant literary merit is not to say anything of which Garvey himself was unaware. From a purely literary standpoint, he inspired better poetry than he himself produced. He even expressed doubts as to whether some of his poetical efforts actually measured up to real poetry. Even so, however, he could still justify the attempt, for he saw his verse as an important supplementary vehicle for propagating his ideas. And these are the ideas upon which the world's greatest Pan-African movement was built.

Garvey's most extensive commentary on his own poetry came in the 1935 foreword to the third edition of his *Tragedy of White Injustice.* He conceived the object of this "little pamphlet" as "that of giving the Negro a thought, with the hope of inspiring him toward the freeing of himself from the ugly octopus of race prejudice and exploitation, which has been devouring him in his universal association with certain members of the white race."

"All good psychologists," Garvey declared, knew that to set a person thinking was to establish the precondition for possible action. His object was therefore to get the Blackman "to accomplish much for himself out of his own thoughtfulness." He considered this work to be strictly speaking neither verse nor "orthodox prose," but rather "a kind of mean[s] adopted for the purpose of conveying the desired thought."

Garvey evidently wished to emphasize this point, for he reiterated it in the final sentence of his brief foreword. He said, "It must be remembered that this is not an attempt at poetry: it is just a peculiar style of using facts as they impress me as I go through the pages of history and as I look and note the conduct of the white race."

However one chooses to describe *The Tragedy of White Injustice* and the other lines that follow—poetry or unorthodox prose—they nevertheless represent an important part of the corpus of a great man's ideas.

I would like to thank the following persons—Marcus Garvey, Jr. and Mrs. Ida Repole for permission to reprint those poems copyrighted by Marcus Garvey and Amy Jacques Garvey; Kwabena O. Prempeh, international organizer of the Universal Negro Improvement Association and the late Mr. A. L. Crawford, former president of the Brooklyn, New York, UNIA, for an original copy of the *Selections from the Poetic Meditations of Marcus Garvey;* Paul Coates of Black Classic Press for a reprint copy of the third edition of *The Tragedy of White Injustice.*

Tony Martin
Wellesley, Massachusetts
February 1983

# 1

## The Tragedy of White Injustice

## The Tragedy of White Injustice

### (1)

Lying and stealing is the whiteman's game;
For rights of God nor man he has no shame
(A practice of his throughout the whole world)
At all, great thunderbolts he has hurled;
He has stolen everywhere—land and sea;
A buccaneer and pirate he must be,
Killing all, as he roams from place to place,
Leaving disease, mongrels—moral disgrace.

### (2)

The world's history of him is replete,
From his javelin-bolt to new-built fleet:
Hosts he has robbed and crushed below;
Of friend and neighbor he has made a foe.
From our men and women he made the slave,
Then boastingly he calls himself a brave;
Cowardly, he steals on his trusting prey,
Killing in the dark, then shouts he hoo ray!

### (3)

Not to go back to time pre-historic,
Only when men in Nature used to frolic,
And you will find his big, long murder-list,
Showing the plunderings of his mailed fist;
Africa, Asia and America
Tell the tale in a mournful replica
How tribesmen, Indians and Zulus fell
Fleeing the murdering bandit pell mell.

3

(4)

American Indian tribes were free,
Sporting, dancing, and happy as could be;
Asia's hordes lived then a life their own,
To civilization they would have grown;
Africa's millions laughed with the sun,
In the cycle of man a course to run;
In stepped the white man, bloody and grim,
The light of these people's freedom to dim.

(5)

Coolies of Asiatics they quickly made,
In Africa's blacks they built a world trade,
The Red Indians they killed with the gun,
All else of men and beasts they put to run;
Blood of murderer Cain is on their head,
Of man and beast they mean to kill dead;
A world of their own is their greatest aim,
For which Yellow and Black are well to blame.

(6)

Out of cold old Europe these white men came,
From caves, dens, and holes, without any fame,
Eating their dead's flesh and sucking their blood,
Relics of the Mediterranean flood;
Literature, science and art they stole,
After Africa had measured each pole,
Asia taught them what great learning was,
Now they frown upon what the Coolie does.

(7)

They have stolen, murdered, on their way here,
Leaving desolation and waste everywhere;
Now they boastingly tell what they have done,
Seeing not the bloody crown they have won;

Millions of Blacks died in America,
Coolies, peons, serfs, too, in Asia;
Upon these dead bones Empires they builded,
Parceling out crowns and coronets gilded.

### (8)

Trifling with God's Holy Name and Law,
Mixing Christ's religion that had no flaw,
They have dared to tell us what is right,
In language of death-bullets, gas and might
Only with their brute force they hold us down,
Men of color, Yellow, Red, Black and Brown:
Not a fair chance give they our men to rise,
Christian liars we see in their eyes.

### (9)

With the Bible they go to foreign lands,
Taking Christ and stealth in different hands;
Making of God a mockery on earth,
When of the Holy One there is no dearth:
They say to us: "You, sirs, are the heathen,
"We your brethren—Christian fellowmen,
"We come to tell the story of our God";
When we believe, they give to us the rod.

### (10)

After our confidence they have thus won,
From our dear land and treasure we must run;
Story of the Bible no more they tell,
For our souls redeemed we could go to hell.
Oil, coal and rubber, silver and gold,
They have found in wealth of our lands untold;
Thus, they claim the name of our country, all,
Of us they make then their real foot-ball.

### (11)

If in the land we happen to tarry,
Most of us then become sad and sorry,
For a white man's country they say it is,
And with shot, gas and shell, they prove it his:
What can we do who love the Gracious Lord,
But fight, pray, watch and wait His Holy word:
His second coming we know to be true,
Then, He will greet the white man with his due.

### (12)

This Christ they killed on Calvary's Cross,
After His Person around they did toss:
White men the Savior did crucify,
For eyes not blue, but blood of Negro tie;
Now they worship Him in their churches great,
And of the Holy Ghost they daily prate;
"One God" they say, enough for all mankind,
When in slavery the Blacks they entwined.

### (13)

Their churches lines of demarcation draw;
In the name of Christ there is no such law,
Yet Black and White they have separated,
A Jim Crow God the preachers operated,
Then to Heaven they think they will all go,
When their consciences ought to tell them NO.
God is no respecter of persons great,
So each man must abide his final fate.

### (14)

We'd like to see the white man converted,
And to right and justice be devoted;
Continuing in land-values to lie and steal,
Will bring destruction down upon his heel.

All that the other races want, I see,
Is the right to liberty and be free;
This the selfish white man doesn't want to give;
He alone, he thinks, has the right to live.

### (15)

There shall be a bloody mix-up everywhere;
Of the white man's plunder we are aware:
Men of color the great cause understand,
Unite they must, to protect their own land.
No fool's stand on argument must we make;
Between Heaven and earth an oath we take:
"Our lands to deliver from foreign foes,
Caring not of trials and maudlin woes."

### (16)

The privilege of men to protect home
Was established before the days of Rome.
Many gallant races fought and died,
Alien hordes in triumph thus defied.
Carthage did not crush Ancient Greece
For their believing in the Golden Fleece.
No other race shall kill the sturdy Blacks
If on their tribal gods we turn our backs.

### (17)

From Marathon, Tours, Blenheim and the Marne
A braver courage in man has been born;
Africans died at Thermopylae's Pass,
Standing firm for Persia—men of Brass.
The Black Archers of Ethiopia stood
At Marathon, proving their stern manhood;
Senegalese held their own at Verdun,
Even though their praises are not now sung.

(18)

In the Americas' modern warfare
The Blacks have ever borne their share;
With Cortez, Washington, too, and the rest,
We did for the others our truthful best;
At St. Domingo we struck a clear blow
To show which way the wind may one day go.
Toussaint L'Ouverture was our leader then,
At the time when we were only half-men.

(19)

Italians, Menelik put to chase,
Beating a retreat in uneven haste;
So down the line of history we come,
Black, courtly, courageous and handsome.
No fear have we today of any great men
From Napoleon back to Genghis Khan;
All we ask of men is "Give a square deal,"
Returning to others same right we feel.

(20)

With a past brilliant, noble and grand,
Black men march to the future hand in hand;
We have suffered long from the white man's greed,
Perforce he must change his unholy creed.
Stealing, bullying and lying to all
Will drag him to ignominious fall;
For men are wise—yes, no longer are fools,
To have grafters make of them still cheap tools.

(21)

Each race should be proud and stick to its own,
And the best of what they are should be shown;
This is no shallow song of hate to sing,
But over Blacks there should be no white king.

Every man on his own foothold should stand,
Claiming a nation and a Fatherland!
White, Yellow and Black should make their own laws,
And force no one-sided justice with flaws.

### (22)

Man will bear so much of imposition,
Till he starts a righteous inquisition.
History teaches this as a true fact,
Upon this premise all men do act.
Sooner or later each people take their stand
To fight against the strong, oppressive hand;
This is God's plan, raising man to power,
As over sin and greed He makes him tower.

### (23)

This trite lesson the white man has not learnt,
Waiting until he gets his fingers burnt.
Milleniums ago, when white men slept,
The great torch of light Asia kept.
Africa at various periods shone
Above them all as the bright noonday sun;
Coming from the darkened cave and hut,
The white man opened the gate that was shut.

### (24)

Gradually light bore down upon him,
This ancient savage who was once dim;
When he commenced to see and move around,
He found the book of knowledge on the ground;
Centuries of wonder and achievements
Were cast before him in God's compliments;
But, like the rest, he has now fallen flat,
And must in the Lord's cycle yield for that.

(25)

We shall always be our brother's keeper,
Is the injunction of the Redeemer;
Love and tolerance we must ever show,
If in Grace Divine we would truly grow;
This is the way clear to God's great kingdom—
Not by the death-traps of Argonne or Somme,
When the terrible white man learns this much,
He will save even the African Dutch.

(26)

South Africa has a grave problem now
In reducing the Negro to the plow;
White men are to live in their lazy ease
While the patience of the goodly natives tease;
They make new laws to have Africa white
Precipitating righteous and ready fight:
Around the world they speak of being so just,
Yet, in fact, no lone white man can you trust.

(27)

In Australia the same they have done,
And so, wherever man's confidence won:
This they call the religion of the Christ,
And upon their willing slave try to foist.
Only a part of the world can you fool,
And easily reduce to your foot-stool;
The other one-half is always awake,
And from it you cannot liberty take.

(28)

"And now valiant Black men of the west
Must ably rise to lead and save the rest":
This is the ringing call Africa sounds,
As throughout the Godly world it resounds;

Clansmen! black, educated, virile and true!
Let us prove too that we are loyal blue.
We must win in the blessed fight of love,
Trusting on the Maker of men above.

### (29)

The Christian world is yet to be saved!
Man, since the risen Christ has not behaved!
Wanton, reckless, wicked, he still remains,
Causing grief, sorrow, tears and human pains!
Can we show the Godly light to anyone
Seeking for earnest truth while marching on?
If so, friend, let us tell you now and here,
For love, freedom, justice let's all prepare!

### (30)

God in His Glorious Might is coming,
Wonderful signs He is ever showing,
Unrest, earthquakes, hurricanes, floods and storms
Are but revelations of Heavenly Forms:
The proud white scientist thinks he is wise
But the Black man's God comes in true disguise,
God is sure in the rumbling earthquake,
When He is ready, the whole world will shake.

### (31)

The Armageddon is gathering now;
The sign is on every oppressed man's brow:
The whites who think they are ever so smart
Do not know other men can play their part:
When the opportune time is almost here
Black, Yellow and Brown will be ev'rywhere,
In union of cause they'll stand together
And storms of the bully boldly weather.

### (32)

Their gases and shots, and their rays of death,
Shall only be child's play—a dream of Seth,
For out of the clear, sleeping minds of ages,
Wonders shall be written on history's pages:
Our buried arts and sciences then shall rise,
To show how for centuries we were wise:
Silent tongues we kept, by God's true command,
Until of us, action, He did demand.

### (33)

Under the canopy of Nature's law
We shall unitedly and bravely draw.
On the plains of God's green Amphitheatre,
Swords, in rhythm with Divine Meter:
Jehovah's Day will have surely come,
With Angelic strains and Seraphic hum:
The Guides of Heaven will direct the way,
Keeping us from wandering far astray.

### (34)

Like around the high walls of Jericho,
March we, as Rio speeds through Mexico:
Trumpets loud will the Guiding Angels blow.
As scatter the enemy to-and-fro:
Heaven will have given us a battle cry:
"Oh Brave Soldiers you shall never die":
Rally to the command of Heaven's King,
As Cherubim to Him your tidings bring.

### (35)

See the deadly clash of arms! Watch! They fall!
There is stillness!—It is the funeral pall!
A sad requiem now is to be sung!
Not by Angels, but in their human tongue!

The cruel masters of yest'rday are done!
From the fields of battle they have run!
A brand new world of justice is to be!
"You shall be a true brother unto me!"

### (36)

This is a forecast of God's wrath:
White man, will you turn from the evil path?
There is still hope for you, among the good:
If you will seek the bigger-brotherhood:
Stop your tricks, frauds, lying and stealing,
And settle down to fair and square dealing;
If not, prepare yourself for gloomy hell,
As God announces the sorrowing knell.

### (37)

Your lies, to us called diplomacy,
Are known by us, a brazen phantasy;
You imprison men for crimes not so great,
While on your silly wisdom you do prate.
The masses are soberly watching you;
They know that you are false and so untrue.
The laborers of your race you oppress,
As well as black and other men you distress.

### (38)

If you were wise you'd read between the lines
Of feudal isms and others of old times.
Men have fought against ugly royal gods,
Burying them 'neath European sods.
Such to heartless masters the people do,
From Syracuse to bloody Waterloo;
Wonderful lessons for any sober man,
Who worships not idols or the god Pan.

(39)

In the vicious order of things today,
The poor, suffering black man has no say;
The plot is set for one 'gainst the other,
With organization they mustn't bother.
"If one should show his head as a leader,
Whom we cannot use, the rest to pilfer,
We shall discredit him before his own,
And make of him a notorious clown."

(40)

"In Africa we have plans to match him,
While the native Chiefs of their lands we trim;
The Blacks schooled in England are too smart,
On the I BETTER THAN YOU scheme we'll start,
And have them thinking away from the rest;
This philosophy for them is best—
Easier then we can rob the good lands
And make ourselves rich without soiled hands."

(41)

"We will so keep from them the 'NEGRO WORLD'
That no news they'll have of a flag unfurled;
Should they smuggle copies in, and we fail,
We will send the sly agents all to jail."
This is the white man's plan across the sea.
Isn't this wily and vicious as can be?
In other lands they have things arranged
Differently, yet they have never changed.

(42)

In America they have Colored to tell
What they know of the rest, whose rights they sell;
The Blacks they do try to keep always down,
But in time they will reap what they have sown.

No Negro's good life is safe in the STATES
If he tries to be honest with his mates;
In politics he must sell at the polls,
To suit the white man in his many roles.

### (43)

The West Indian whites are tricky, too;
They have schemes curved like the horse's shoe:
There is only one opening for the black—
Three other sides are close up to his back;
Hence he never gets a chance to look in
Whilst staring at the world of mortal sin.
Yes, this is the game they play everywhere,
Leaving the Negro to gloom and despair.

### (44)

And now, white man, can we reason with you,
For each race in the world to give it due?
Africa for Africans is most right;
Asia for Asiatics is light;
To Europe for the Europeans,
America for the Americans:
This is the doctrine of the goodly Klan,
Now fighting for the alien ban.

### (45)

Blacks do not hate you because you are white;
We believe in giving to all men right;
Some we do keep for ourselves to protect,
Knowing it as a virtue to select.
We are willing to be friends of mankind,
Pulling all together with none behind,
Growing in sane goodness and fellowship,
Choosing but the Almighty to worship.

### (46)

Let justice prevail, at home and abroad;
Cease over the weak your burdens to lord;
You're but mortal man, like the rest of us—
Of this happy truth we need make no fuss.
All Nature's kindly gifts are justly ours—
Suns, oceans, trees, to pretty flowers—
So we need not doubt the marvelous fact
That God has given to each man his tract.

### (47)

The common thief now steals a crust of bread,
The law comes down upon his hungry head;
The haughty land robber steals continents,
With men, oil, gold, rubber and all contents.
The first you say is a hopeless convic',
While the latter escapes the law by trick;
That grave, one-sided justice will not do—
The poor call for consideration, too.

### (48)

The rich white man starts the unholy war,
Then from the line of action he keeps far;
He pushes to the front sons of the poor,
There to do battle, die, suffer galore,
As the guns rage, liberty loans they raise,
And in glorious tones sing freedom's praise.
This is the method to gain them more wealth,
Then, after vict'ry they practice great stealth.

### (49)

Those who make wars should first go to the front,
And of gas, shot and shell bear there the brunt:
In first lines of action they are all due,
If to their country and people they are true:

When this is demanded in right of all,
There will be no more deadly cannon ball:
The downtrodden poor whites and blacks should join
And prevent rich whites our rights to purloin.

(50)
Weeping mothers, tricked in patriotism,
Send their sons to fight for liberalism:
Into most far off lands they go with pride,
Thinking right and God be on their side:
When they get into the bloody trenches,
They find of lies they had awful drenches:
The people they were all supposed to kill,
Like themselves, had gotten of lies their fill.

(51)
In the private club and drawing room,
White schemes are hatched for the nation's doom:
Speculators, grafters, bankers—all,
With politicians join to hasten the fall,
By stealing rights from other citizens,
As if they weren't fit or true denizens:
How awful is this daring story
That we tell to men young and hoary.

(52)
Crooked lawyers, friends and politicians,
Corrupt the morals of the good nations:
Between them and others, fly plots they make,
Innocent citizens' money to take;
From banks they find out your real account,
Then have you indicted on legal count:
Large fees they charge, to have you surely broke,
Then, to prison you go—what a sad joke!

### (53)

The white man controls cable and wireless,
Connections by ships with force and duress:
He keeps black races of the world apart,
So to his schemes they may not be smart:
"There shall be no Black Star Line Ships," he says,
"For that will interfere with our crooked ways:
"I'll disrupt their business and all their plans,
"So they might not connect with foreign lands."

### (54)

Black women are raped by the lordly white,
In colonies, the shame ne'er reaching light:
In other countries abuses are given,
Shocking to morality and God's Heaven.
Hybrids and mongrels are the open result,
Which the whites give us as shameful insult:
How can they justify this? None can tell;
Yet, crimes of the blacks are rung with a bell.

### (55)

White men newspapers subsidize and own,
For to keep them on their racial throne:
Editors are slaves to fool the public,
Reporters tell the lie and pull the trick;
The papers support only what they want,
Yet truth, fair play, and justice, daily flaunt:
They make criminals out of honest men,
And force judges to send them to the Pen.

### (56)

Capitalists buy up all blank space
To advertise and hold the leading place
For to influence public opinion
And o'er Chief-editors show dominion.

The average man is not wise to the scheme,
He, the reformer, must now redeem;
This isn't a smooth or very easy job,
For, you, of your honor and name, they'll rob.

### (57)

The bankers employ men to shoot and kill,
When we interfere with their august will;
They take the savings of deaf, dumb and poor,
Gamble with it here and on foreign shore:
In oil, gold, rum, rubber they speculate,
Then bring their foreign troubles upon the State:
Friends in Government they control at will;
War they make, for others, our sons to kill.

### (58)

The many foundations of researches,
And the foreign missions and their churches,
Are organized to catch the mild converts
Who don't understand the way of perverts.
Our wealth when discovered by researchers,
In lands of the Native occupiers
Is surveyed and marked to the river's rim
Till they dislodge a Premprey or Abd-El-Krim.

### (59)

It is not freedom from prison we seek;
It is freedom from the big thieves we meet;
All life is now a soulless prison cell,
A wild suspense between heaven and hell:
Selfish, wicked whites have made it so;
To the Author and Finisher we'll go,
Carrying our sad cares and many wrongs
To Him in prayers and holy songs.

### (60)

This is the game that is played all around,
Which is sure one day to each race rebound:
The world is gone mad with the money craze,
Leaving the poor man in a gloomy haze:
There must be world reorganization,
To save the masses from exploitation;
The cry is for greater democracy.
A salvation from man's hypocrisy.

### (61)

Out in this heartless, bitter oasis
There's now very little of human bliss;
The cold capitalists and money sharks
Have made life unsafe, like ocean barks.
The once dear, lovely Garden of Eden
Has become the sphere of men uneven;
The good God created but an equal pair,
Now man has robbed others of their share.

### (62)

Shall there be freedom of liberal thought?
No; the white man has all agencies bought—
Press, pulpit, law and every other thing—
Hence o'er public opinion he reigns king.
This is indisputable, glaring fact;
You may find it out with a little tact.
College tutors and presidents are paid,
So that in universities schemes are laid.

### (63)

Cleopatra, Empress Josephine,
Were black mongrels like of the Philippine:
Mixtures from black and other races they,
Yet "true" the white man's history will not say

To those who seek the light of pure knowledge
In the inquiring world, school or college.
Napoleon fell for a Negro woman;
So did the Caesars, and the Great Roman.

### (64)

Anthony lost his imperial crown
To escape Cleo's fascinating frown.
This truth the New Negro knows very well,
And to his brothers in darkness he'll tell.
No one can imprison the brain of man—
That was never intended in God's plan;
You may persecute, starve, even debase—
That will not kill truth nor virtue efface.

### (65)

The white man now enjoys his "Vanity Fair";
He thinks of self and not of others care—
Fratricidal course, that to hell doth lead—
This is poison upon which the gentry feed.
Blacks should study physics, chemistry, more,
While the gold God all such sinners adore;
This is no idle prattle talk to you;
It has made the banners red, white and blue.

### (66)

Out of the clear of God's Eternity
Shall rise a kingdom of Black Fraternity;
There shall be conquests o'er militant forces;
For as man proposes, God disposes.
Signs of retribution are on every hand:
Be ready, black men, like Gideon's band.
They may scoff and mock at you today,
But get you ready for the awful fray.

### (67)

In the fair movement of God's Abounding Grace
There is a promised hope for the Negro race;
In the sublimest truth of prophecy,
God is to raise them to earthly majesty,
Princes shall come out of Egypt so grand,
The noble black man's home and Motherland,
The Psalmist spoke in holy language clear,
As Almighty God's triune will declare.

### (68)

In their conceit they see not their ruin;
You soldiers of trust, be up and doing!
Remember Belshazzar's last joyous feast,
And Daniel's vision of the Great Beast!
"Weighed in the balances and found wanting"
Is the Tekel to which they are pointing.
This interpretation of the Prophet
Black men shall never in their dreams forget.

### (69)

The resplendent rays of the morning sun
Shall kiss the Negro's life again begun;
The music of God's rhythmic natural law
Shall stir Afric's soul without Divine flaw.
The perfume from Nature's rosy hilltops
Shall fall on us spiritual dewdrops.
Celestial beings shall know us well,
For, by goodness, in death, with them we'll dwell.

### (70)
### AND HOW SAD A FINIS!

With battleship, artillery and gun
White men have put all God's creatures to run;
Heaven and earth they have often defied,
Taking no heed of the rebels that died.

God can't be mocked in this daring way,
So the evil ones shall sure have their day.
"You may rob, you may kill, for great fame,"
So says the white man, FOR THIS IS HIS GAME.


## Hail! United States of Africa!

Hail! United States of Africa—free!
Hail! Motherland most bright, divinely fair!
State in perfect sisterhood united,
Born of truth; mighty thou shalt ever be.

Hail! Sweet land of our father's noble kin!
Let joy within thy bounds be ever known;
Friend of the wandering poor, and helpless, thou,
Light to all, such as freedom's reigns within.

From Liberia's peaceful western coast
To the foaming Cape at the southern end,
There's but one law and sentiment sublime,
One flag, and its emblem of which we boast.

The Nigerias are all united now,
Sierra Leone and the Gold Coast, too.
Gambia, Senegal, not divided,
But in one union happily bow.

The treason of the centuries is dead,
All alien whites are forever gone;
The glad home of Sheba is once more free,
As o'er the world the black man raised his head.

Bechuanaland, a State with Kenya,
Members of the Federal Union grand,
Send their greetings to sister Zanzibar,
And so does laughing Tanganyika.

Over in Grand Mother Mozambique,
The pretty Union Flag floats in the air,
She is sister to good Somaliland,
Smiling with the children of Dahomey.

Three lusty cheers for old Basutoland,
Timbuctoo, Tunis and Algeria,
Uganda, Kamerun, all together
Are in the Union with Nyasaland.

We waited long for fiery Morocco,
Now with Guinea and Togo she has come,
All free and equal in the sisterhood,
Like Swazi, Zululand and the Congo.

There is no state left out of the Union—
The East, West, North, South, including Central,
Are in the nation, strong forever,
Over blacks in glorious dominion.

Hail! United States of Africa—free!
Country of the brave black man's liberty;
State of greater nationhood thou hast won,
A new life for the race is just begun.


### Africa For The Africans

Say! Africa for the Africans,
Like America for the Americans:
This the rallying cry for a nation,
Be it in peace or revolution.

Blacks are men, no longer cringing fools;
They demand a place, not like weak tools;
But among the world of nations great
They demand a free self-governing state.

Hurrah! Hurrah! Great Africa wakes;
She is calling her sons, and none forsakes,
But to colors of the nation runs,
Even though assailed by enemy guns.

Cry it loud, and shout it long, hurrah!
Time has changed, so hail! New Africa!
We are now awakened, rights to see;
We shall fight for dearest liberty.

Mighty kingdoms have been truly reared
On the bones of blackmen, facts declared;
History tells this awful, pungent truth,
Africa awakes to her rights forsooth.

Europe cries to Europeans, ho!
Asiatics claim Asia, so
Australia for Australians,
And Africa for the Africans.

Blackmen's hands have joined now together,
They will fight and brave all death's weather,
Motherland to save, and make her free,
Spreading joy for all to live and see.

None shall turn us back, in freedom's name,
We go marching like to men of fame
Who have given laws and codes to kings,
Sending evil flying on crippled wings.

Blackmen shall in groups reassemble,
Rich and poor and the great and humble:
Justice shall be their rallying cry,
When millions of soldiers pass us by.

Look for that day, coming, surely soon,
When the sons of Ham will show no coon

Could the mighty deeds of valor do
Which shall bring giants for peace to sue.

Hurrah! Hurrah! Better times are near;
Let us front the conflict and prepare;
Greet the world as soldiers, bravely true:
"Sunder not," Africa shouts to you.

# 2

## Selections from the Poetic Meditations of Marcus Garvey (1927)

### You and Me

When we think of all the care
　　That made life's burden great,
We long for the passing year
　　To close our sad book of Fate:
But if we should stop a while,
　　And think once the other way,
Life would be just all a smile,
　　As we go on day by day.

We should never make day night
　　For to darken life's good view;
Round that turning is the light
　　That shines as a guide to you:
Think of all that's really good,
　　Then make it your daily rule;
Smile with Nature's Brotherhood,
　　And none make your footstool.

A proverb for every day,
　　And one more for each good night,
Should make life so pleasant, yea,
　　Would lead us to live all right:
Turn not from sane rectitude,
　　But make life just like a song;
Go ye not with the multitude
　　To any path that's wholly wrong.

October 24, 1927

## Christ the Way

Oh, with the Spirit as of old,
    I chant a prayer to my God;
The Being, precious, more than gold
    That Croesus has ever had.

I lift my soul to Him above,
    And sing the angel's happy praise;
The song of life in joy of love
    That men from earth to Heaven raise.

There's joy in Paradise for me,
    Although a weary child of sin;
The penitent on Calv'ry's tree
    May find the way to enter in.

My hopes are good, in Christ, the Lord;
    On Him I rest my cares of heart;
He will so bridge the Heavenly Ford
    To show the way ere I depart.

October 8, 1927

## Let Us Know

O, thou profound, eternal blue,
    God's mystic arch of heaven-land!
Art thou not veiling spirit hue,
    And hiding the angelic band?
Jehovah! so move this veil,
    That we may see the throne of light,
From which St. Gabriel brought the "Hail"
    To Mary, on that Holy night!

We've slumbered much in darkness here,
    And now we seek more light from Thee:
We feel that peace is reigning there—
    Beyond the clouds, o'er land and sea.
The mystery of eternal life
    Provokes the soul's sad tedium;
We faint beneath this mortal strife,
    And long to join the angels' hum.

Forgive us, Lord, if we have erred,
    In asking this before our time;
We only sought the light, and aired
    Our souls to tunes of spiritual rhyme;
For death has been a puzzle here;
    Some say we live forever on,
Some say we go from life nowhere;
    To tell us right, Thou art the One!

We wait on Thee, great God above!
    But let the message come today;
We sing Thy praise, and Thee we love,
    As to Thee, Father, do we pray:
Let Michael come in glory great,
    To teach us all that we should do;
And then we'll know our rightful fate,
    In worship to the Son and You.

October 29, 1927


## The Last Farewell

Good-bye, my friend, in death we part,
    To meet in realms more glorious:
A void I feel deep in my heart,
    For much there was of love in us:

To see you go is awful pain,
    For thou hast been a world to me;
But we shall meet for good again,
    To see the light that hallows thee.

This death is only transient;
    It leads to brighter and new vales,
So wonderful, munificent,
    As prophets tell in holy tales:
Go thou and wait for me a while,
    And rest at God's fair borderland,
There with the angels you will smile,
    In welcome to the saintly band.

Good-bye, my love, my truest friend;
    All else in life for me to do
Was done ere I in grief attend
    To say the last farewell to you:
The sod has covered you from view,
    But memory dear shall linger still,
And I shall think in heart more true
    Of all your good, and not of ill.

October 27, 1927

## Why Disconsolate?

Oh, traveler, disconsolate!
    Thine heart may yet in solace be,
So brood ye not as if from Fate
    Ignoble thou canst not be free.
Let's journey to the heights of love,
    And cast behind the fears of death;
There is no death in life above,
    For man is truly spiritual breath.

You are an entity of Grace
    Divine, yes, partly God in One:
Your image is divine in race,
    Although you may be mortal man.
Go seek the knowledge of the law,
    Go make yourself the lord of earth;
See then the light that Moses saw,
    That gave him vision of this worth!

To be yourself in triumph great,
    You must the world in truth subdue:
Stamp out the evil thought of fate,
    And manly courage then pursue:
The vineyards of the world are yours;
    Go ye and have your rightful share,
For Nature opened all her doors
    To you, in love, beyond compare.

October 29, 1927


## Have Faith In Self

Today I made myself in life anew,
    By going to that royal fount of truth,
And searching for the secret of the few
    Whose goal in life and aim is joy forsooth.
I found at last the friend and counsellor
    That taught me all that I in life should know;
It is the soul, the sovereign chancellor,
    The guide and keeper of the good you sow.

I am advised—"Go ye, have faith in self,
    And seek once more the guide that lives in you"—
Much better than the world of sordid pelf,
    Alas! I found the counsel to be true.

Aha! I know right now that I shall see
    The good in life, and be a better man;
I will by thought and deed pull all to me,
    In saving others, yea, every one.

Go down and search yourself awhile in part,
    And tell me all of what you see and hear;
Isn't there something pulling at your heart?
    Tell me the truth and have ye then no fear!
There is a voice that speaks to man, within,
    It is the Soul that longs for you to know
There is no need for you to grope in sin,
    For you in truth and light may ever grow.

October 27, 1927


### The Call of Heaven

I've come to learn the story
Of Jesus in His bright glory;
That home for sinners set so free
By love for you and love for me.

I bow to Thee, Son most Holy;
In truth Thou art King of Glory.
So save my soul and make me good
That I may be where Eli stood.

Thy journey through grim Bethany
Led to the Cross' sad agony;
But now Thou art the Lord of Host,
The Father, Son and Holy Ghost.

Now send to me, Light of Glory,
The message good, true and holy;

For I am ready now for home,
No longer in this vale to roam.

October 8, 1927

### Death's Pleasure

Death is no terror, friend!
    It's a sublime sleep
That lulls the weary home
    To rest—not to weep:
It is the solace of God—
    A message for you
From those friends, gone before,
    Those whose love is true.

The dream called death is not
    The pain that you fear;
It's an ecstacy
    Beyond man's compare;
'Tis life's joy—that's called
    The Eternal Fair.

November 10, 1927

### The Bearers

We are the bearers of the world's bright torch
    To light our civilization as we go:
No one should fall or lodge at darkness' porch;
    Right well we teach the people all to know:
There's much for us to do in toil of love,
    In helping others as we climb the heights;
It is for us to reach and lift above
    Those who are struggling up through gloomy nights.

Our beaming standard is the Cross of Christ,
    The same that Simon bore, and fainted not;
Up through the age we will this emblem hoist,
    To falter neither a tittle nor a jot:
The cause of men is dear to us alway;
    For right and truth we stand, most firm, as one.
And so we'll battle on from day to day,
    In fighting for the noble aims of man.

'Tis true the world is reckless, vile and tough;
    But there is always room for doing good:
There never can of goodness be enough,
    In blessing Nature's wanton brotherhood;
Will you now join the faithful, sturdy band,
    To make a better home for man to live?
Will you now stretch to me the other hand,
    And state—"As freely I receive, I give?"

October 26, 1927

### The Little Minds

The little minds that're in the world you know
    Are makers of most troubles that you see;
So small in vision they will ever sow
    Confusion over land and foreign sea:
In politics they reign supreme and great,
    To fool the innocent and rob their rights,
Thus spreading o'er the land vile human hate,
    To end in death and wasteful battle flights.

So selfish are the politicians now
    That neither soul nor body need not hope,
If to their ways and schemes you do not bow
    With cheer, to fall in line with party- dope:

These rascals have in hand the right of way,
   So gained by fraud and many studied tricks,
And then, to keep the populace at bay,
   They threaten all good men with "legal bricks."

No wonder then the world is gone to hell,
   For good men have no place to move nor sit;
This needs no vision of a William Tell,
   For you can feel or look just straight at it:
A wonderful reform for all must be,
   To save the world for good, and make men right;
There must be liberty for you and me,
   For this, all sober minds should strive and fight.

October 26, 1927

## Man to Man

Yes, man to man is so unjust
Until we know not whom to trust;
For we have made of life a lie,
In treating man less than fly:
To tell the reason why it's so,
Into history we must go,
Revealing crime, just after crime,
From Cain and Abel to this time.

Our God made man in perfect form,
And to the standard to conform;
But in his ways of self alone
He crushed the good and built a throne:
A regal personage is he,
As proud and selfish as can be;
Forgetting God he robs and kills,
And lays the course of human ills.

Is there no help that we can give
To brighten life in truth to live?
Yes, there is much for you to do
In treating man as Christ did you:
If we should change the old bad way,
The good would shine in us each day,
Then life would be a happy dream,
A radiant, fair morning beam.

October 25, 1927

## Music In My Soul

There's music in my soul today,
    A joy of heart not there before:
This state of conscience I relay
    To rich and proud and meek and poor.
There's music in my happy Soul:
    From Heaven's realm doth truly flow
This music in my happy Soul,
    My conscience tells me rightly so.

My song of joy I sing to you:
    Let peace and love forever be
Among ye men of every hue,
    Of every land and charted sea.

I crave no other fortune great,
    But joy to live in peace with God;
My hopes are fixed on His Estate,
    In faith so true as prophets had.

This music in my soul today
　　I spread in truth with love unfurled;
On waves of cheer it goes, I pray,
　　To reach around the belted world.

August 23, 1927


## The Start

Today I start my life for good;
　　I am determined now to find
The value of my real manhood;
　　And not to travel as if blind.
I am yet young in age and hope;
　　I shall so think and do aright,
Things human, and, all in my scope,
　　To make of life a shining light.

There shall be no mistake in plan,
　　For time does not permit to lose,
And win again, the race of man;
　　Hence, now I start, and rightly choose.
I shall not travel wild to find
　　That I have fallen almost flat,
Then rise to weep and leave behind
　　That I a coward was for that.

So find yourself in early age,
　　To know what you shall be in life;
Then go and write on hist'ry's page
　　The vict'ries of your daily strife;
For every man is battling you,

To cross the plain, with haste to win—
And hoist the flag in colors blue—
    Then show the world where he has been.

October 31, 1927

## The World and You

The world is cold and terrible, you know,
Experience has taught the trav'ler so:
We journey from our native coast to coast,
To find little of which to gloat or boast.

However, if we trust our Conscience's Guide,
We sure shall have the truth and God beside:
This Urge of destiny is Nature's light,
It ne'er shall go astray if followed right.

October 18, 1927

## Find Yourself

All men have troubles of their own,
    And burdens great to bear each day,
So keep your tales of woe, and frown
    At all the ills that come your way:
You need not harbor sorry pain,
    And make the world a living hell;
For there is naught in this to gain;
    The wisdom of the age will tell.

The other fellow does not care
    A bit, what ails and worries you;
In life he has to pay his fare
    In living right as you should do:

He bears his burdens like a man,
    And smiles with every wind;
There is a reason why he can
    Thus master right his soul and mind.

To conscience go in quiet mood.
    And find yourself each morn anew;
Feed thou upon the psychic food
    That makes the gods in mortal hue:
This is the way that men are great—
    All those who smile with Nature's laws—
So then, why brood and curse your fate?
    Brace up and strike against your flaws!

October 26, 1927


## The Love Amie

### (Dedicated to Mrs. Amy Jacques Garvey)

I wandered far in life's stern way
To seek the good of every day;
But fell among the thieves of Thane,
Who tried to rob my honest name.

I found no brotherhood in man;
But here and there a vicious clan;
No truth, no love, no justice find
Their way into these groups unkind.

But you have been a light to me,
A fond and dear, and true Amie;
So what care I for falsest friend,
When on your love I can depend.

To steal one's wealth is always trash,
O'er which some men are ne'er abash;

But then to steal and blot a name,
It takes the courage of a Thane,

But all they do is only nought,
Because the battle has been fought,
And I have won your love, Amie,
The greatest treasure I can see.

October 31, 1927


## White and Black

The white man held the blacks as slaves,
And bled their souls in living death;
Bishops and priests, and kings themselves,
Preached that the law was right and just;
And so the people worked and died,
And crumbled into material dust.
Good God! The scheme is just the same
Today, between the black and white
Races of men, who gallop after fame.
Can'st Thou not change this bloody thing,
And make white people see the truth
That over blacks must be their king,
Not white, but of their somber hue,
To rule a nation of themselves?

October 31, 1927


## Love's Morning Star

I've waited patiently for you,
    And now you come to make me glad;
I shall be ever good and true,
    And be the dearest, sweetest dad.

You cheer my life with every smile,
    And make me feel much like a bird
That flits and sings just all the while
    Such songs as you have always heard.

You are the beacon light, my dear,
    That guides me on the happy way;
Such love as yours I would not share,
    But treasure in my heart all day.

I dream of you each eve and morn;
    I picture you from distance far,
And everywhere, where love is born,
    You are the brightest morning star.

October 31, 1927


## God In Man

O weary son of sorrow great!
    How apt art thou to bow and grieve,
And count all things thy solemn fate,
    As if thou canst not self retrieve!

May I not tell the story true
    Of that Eternal Force that is—
The Force that makes the world and you;
    The Force that rules and ever lives?

Thou art the living force in part,
    The Spirit of the Mighty I;
The God of Heaven and your heart
    Is Spirit that can never die.

You're what you are in heart and mind,
    Because you will it so to be;

The man who tries himself to find,
    Is light to all, and great is he.

In each and every one is God,
    In everything atomic life;
There is no death beneath the sod,
    This fact, not knowing, brings the strife.

August 26, 1927


### The Black Woman

Black queen of beauty, thou hast given color to the world!
Among other women thou art royal and the fairest!
Like the brightest of jewels in the regal diadem,
Shin'st thou, Goddess of Africa, Nature's purest emblem!

Black men worship at thy virginal shrine of truest love,
Because in thine eyes are virtue's steady and holy mark,
As we see in no other, clothed in silk or fine linen,
From ancient Venus, the Goddess, to mythical Helen.

When Africa stood at the head of the elder nations,
The Gods used to travel from foreign lands to look at
    thee:
On couch of costly Eastern materials, all perfumed,
Reclined thee, as in thy path flow'rs were strewn—
    sweetest that bloomed.

Thy transcendent marvelous beauty made the whole
    world mad,
Bringing Solomon to tears as he viewed thy comeliness;
Anthony and the elder Ceasars wept at thy royal feet,
Preferring death than to leave thy presence, their foes
    to meet.

You, in all ages, have attracted the adoring world,
And caused many a bloody banner to be unfurled:
You have sat upon exalted and lofty eminence,
To see a world fight in your ancient African defense.

Today you have been dethroned, through the weakness of
    your men,
While, in frenzy, those who of yore craved your smiles
    and your hand—
Those who were all monsters and could not with love
    approach you—
Have insulted your pride and now attack your good virtue.

Because of disunion you became mother of the world,
Giving tinge of robust color to five continents,
Making a greater world of millions of colored races,
Whose claim to beauty is reflected through our black
    faces.

From the handsome Indian to European brunette,
There is a claim for that credit of their sunny beauty
That no one can e'er to take from thee, O Queen of all
    women
Who have borne trials and troubles and racial burden.

Once more we shall, in Africa, fight and conquer for you,
Restoring the pearly crown that proud Queen Sheba did
    wear:
Yea, it may mean blood, it may mean death; but still we
    shall fight,
Bearing our banners to Vict'ry, men of Afric's might.

Superior Angels look like you in Heaven above,
For thou art fairest, queen of the seasons, queen of our
    love:
No condition shall make us ever in life desert thee,
Sweet Goddess of the ever green land and placid blue sea.

February 28, 1927

### The Bravest Soul

The toil of life is never ending;
    It passes from one stage to others;
We live beneath its sombre bending,
    And ape the customs of our fathers.

We glory in its radiant joys,
    And smile with the everlasting sun;
This eternal change that man employs,
    Has been so from Adam's day begun.

The bravest soul truly conquers all,
    In seeing God in our fellow man;
This planet is just a spinning ball
    Of God's wondrous spiritual plan.

In this life we may know no better;
    But in death we pass to Spirit Land,
Where the Soul is free from all fetter,
    To join God in His creative hand.

August 22, 1927


### The City Storm

I stood at attention to see—there was an angry thunder-
    clap!
A natural manifestation of the ugly clouds above!
Proud man was all in excitement, questioning the mean-
    ing of darkness
That surrounded him on every side, from mother earth
    to heaven!
Men were looking through closed windows with stares
    of anxiety!

Mothers were seeking their children for closer union of love!
All motive power in the city had come to a sudden stop!
There was nothing cheerful, only gloom and prehistoric
   weirdness!

It was not the end of all time, nor the hour for Gabriel's
   horn:
It was atmospheric change, caused through elemental
   moodiness,
That sometimes makes us feel that our sciences are but
   speculations,
And the majesty of man, feeble, as his finite intellect:
Yet, there was a fear and trembling as I observed it all
   around!
Hearts were searched and prayers were offered in devout
   holiness!
Everyone thought it was the end of the world, the great
   Judgment morn—
The final visitation of God upon man's vain damnations!

I wondered to myself when I saw the weakness of my
   brother
In the moment of apparent danger and infinite distress,
How is it he finds heart to enslave the rest of his fellowmen,
When conscience must tell him withal, we are in reality
   one?
Those heavy clouds or roaring Heaven did not gather all
   in vain!
On that day millions saw the evil of their fellows to oppress,
The commonness of love and punishment from the Everlasting Father
Who saves cities, nations and peoples for even the
   righteous ten!

After several blasts of thunder had shaken the trembling
    earth,
The rain from the very clouds burst through in torrential
    showers!
Again there was a sudden breaking of the angry elements!
A stillness, as of death, seemed to reign on every hand
    and shadow!
The sun, in munificent glory shone radiantly once more;
Everything was refreshed, from the green grass to the
    rosy flowers!
It was as if Nature had served her elemental sacraments,
To give new life to the ancient hill, dale, mountain and
    meadow!

But I was satisfied that in the approach of death, men
    unite
To shield themselves by thought and deed from the dread
    and ominous terror!
This was only a storm with its currents of electricity!
Yet the whole populace was aroused to see man's finite
    weakness,
To realize that in the midst of life we are subjects of
    death,
Children of an understanding Source, hidden beyond
    Nature's mirror!
Whether of men we be divided in Yellow, Brown, Black
    or White,
We shall pass from life to the mysterious eternity!

February 25, 1927

### Man's Immortality

Eternal is my lease on life,
If courage I can find to live.
My soul and mind are both in one,

And Nature but my elder self,
Of all I see I am the lord,
Including earth and stars and sea:
From time immemorial I'd been
A part of Almighty God.

He was the Other Self of me,
The All in One, and I a part.
There is no life without my own,
And there's no life without the God:
He is the Source of all you see
Divine, but I a part of Him.

September 14, 1927


### The Wicked Dies

There's a plot for you and one for me,
    Out in God's acre, that's lying by;
You needn't think I cannot also see
    That the wicked shall most surely die.

In the resurrection men shall rise—
Not those, steeped in sin and lies,
But the souls of love for good and truth
Shall blossom forth in spiritual youth.

October 18, 1927


### Merry Christmas

Christmas has a charm so dear,
Coming once for every year,
Bringing Christ in thought anew
With my greeting true to you.

For the everlasting truths
Men may differ in their views;
Still, at Xmas, it's all right
"Merry Christmas" to recite.

October 4, 1927


## A Summer's Dream

As I lay asleep at midnight,
    A thought came stealing over me:
A shadow of a great disaster,
    The passing of my Love at sea.

I heard the chimes of Angelus,
    It sounded sad but ringing clear;
I had a glimpse of dear heaven,
    For my Love was a-going there.

The ship was lost in the ocean,
    As the storm had raged and past;
Every soul was clothed in sadness,
    But my Love was firm to the last.

I stretched my arms out to rescue,
    But my Love was already gone:
A burning light stopped my vision,
    It was like shining glare at morn.

There were Angels in the Heavens,
    And sunny flowers strewn around;
The singing of Royal Cherubs
    Had a pleasing Heavenly sound.

I can almost see how clearly,
    There is a passage made above;
The angels are a-welcoming
    The spirit of my dearest Love.

I am left with my dreams, alone,
    In a cold world of sin and care,
For my Love is gone forever,
    With happy Angels, bliss to share.

I tried to enter into Heaven,
    But the gates were closed to me;
The Guardian of my destiny
    Had not then set my spirit free.

I struggled still with the vision,
    For it was a-torturing me;
My Love was taken to Heaven,
    And the sweet face I could not see.

At last I came to my senses,
    I found it was a summer's dream;
My Love was still right beside me,
    A creature perfect as could seem.

February 24, 1927


### Vision of Niagara

I stood at Niagara's Falls today,
    And viewed the wond'rous work of God;
The mighty river flowing by right o'way,
    Yes, dashing o'er the shaking sod.

I looked again at Nature, and I saw
    That God was everywhere in view:
The roaring river was of ancient law,
    Like sun, and moon and stars—not new.

I learnt a valued lesson then and there,
    To see the waters fall below,
For every drop was like a human tear
    Thus shed in earthly passion's flow.

At once I tossed my head above to look,
    To read the story of the sky;
It was so plain—this Nature's open book—
    I could not doubt, there was no Why!

Again I looked with conscience, easy,
    At Niagara's angry surge—
A living duplicate of Zambezi,
    That beats time's funeral dirge.

And then I knew that all of life is one,
    A march from cradle to the grave;
That every atom is a part of man,
    Who passes—coward and the brave.

November 13, 1927

# 3

## Keep Cool (1927)

## Keep Cool

Suns have set and suns will rise
Upon many gloomy lives;
Those who sit around and say:
"Nothing good comes down our way."
Some say: "What's the use to try,
Life is awful hard and dry."
If they'd bring such news to you,
This is what you ought to do.

*Chorus*

Let no trouble worry you;
Keep cool, keep cool!
Don't get hot like some folk do,
Keep cool, keep cool!
What's the use of prancing high
While the world goes smiling by.
You can win if you would try,
Keep cool, keep cool.

Throw your troubles far away,
Smile a little every day,
And the sun will start to shine,
Making life so true and fine.
Do not let a little care
Fill your life with grief and fear:
Just be calm, be brave and true,
Keep your head and you'll get through.

*Chorus*

Let no trouble worry you;
Keep cool, keep cool!

Just be brave and ever true;
Keep cool, keep cool!
If they'd put you in a flame,
Though you should not bear the blame,
Do not start to raising cane,
Keep cool, keep cool.

# 4

From the *Negro World* (1927)

### The Black Mother

Where can I find love that never changes
  Smiles that are true and always just the same,
Caring not how the fierce tempest rages,
  Willing ever to shield my honored name?

This I find at home, only with Mother,
  Who cares for me with patient tenderness;
She from every human pain would rather
  Save me, and drink the dregs of bitterness.

If on life's way I happen to flounder,
  My true thoughts should be of Mother dear;
She is the rock that ne'er rifts asunder,
  The cry of her child, be it far or near.

This is love wonderful beyond compare;
  It is God's choicest gift to mortal man;
You, who know Mother, in this thought must share,
  For, she, of all, is Angel of your Clan.

My Mother is black, loveliest of all;
  Yes, she is as pure as the new made morn;
Her song of glee is a clear rythmic call
  To these arms of love to which I was born.

I shall never forget you, sweet Mother,
  Where'er in life I may happen to roam;
Thou shalt always be the Fairy Charmer
  To turn my dearest thoughts to things at home.

### The Battle Hymn of Africa

Africa's sun is shining above the horizon clear,
The day for us is rising, for black men far and near;
Our God is in the front line, the heav'nly batallion leads,
Onward, make your banners shine, ye men of noble deeds.

> There's a flag we love so well—
> The red, the black and green,
> Greatest emblem tongues can tell,
> The brightest ever seen.

When pandemonium breaks, the earth will tremble fast,
Nor oceans, seas nor lakes shall save the first or last;
Our suff'ring has been long, our cries to God ascending;
We have counted ev'ry wrong which calls for an amending.

So into battle let us go, with the Cross before;
The Angels, great, from high to low, watch forevermore;
We see the enemy scatter, and watch their ranks divide—
With God there is no fetter for whom He doth provide.

All God's children, in trouble, or burdened down with care,
No matter where, how humble, His love is ever there;
So cheerful let our courage be and rally for the King,
The Saviour, Christ, the Lord, is He, whom angels tidings bring.

Ho, Africa, victorious! See, the foe goes down!
The Christ and Simon lead us to wear the triumphant crown;
Jesus remembers dearly the sacrifice with the cross,
So raise those banners gladly—never to suffer loss!

And so the war is ending, the victor's palm is ours;
Crushed 'neath a sorry bending, like dead, fallen flowers
Thus lay the proud men of the day, all lost, forever,
Where the demons never say to God, "We'll deliver."

## The Dividing Line

There's a dividing line, call it what you may,
It separates the whites from the blacks each day.
Nature made no passing, shadowy blunder
When by race different people set asunder.
You may try to patch a broken fence between,
But one oneness of aim shall e'er be seen;
For peace and happiness, it is the best,
To group them nationally, one from the rest.

Angels are separated by groups and files,
Not because of superiority in lives,
But to maintain heavenly rule and order,
As desired by the Great, Holy Father.
So in this physical, material life
We are thus separated to prevent strife;
Not because we are better than the other,
But for the sake of others not to bother.

Everyone should obey this grand human rule,
And not others to reduce to our footstool.
Justice should be for everyone we meet,
As with charity and fellowship we greet.
This would make a better and happier world
With the banner of peace and love unfurled.
No fair mortal man can think this unkind
If he appreciates the bond of mankind.

# 5

From the *Black Man* Magazine (1933-1939)

### Go And Win

Ye Negroes of the world, another day has come,
To test your worth of racial character;
Your lives and homes, you see, are threatened everywhere;
The time is now for you to do and then to dare.

Your youth must struggle with the facts as they are seen,
And blaze the trail for home and life redeemed:
Your hope, I claim, is in the courage of the time,
So go ye forth and win the battle that's sublime.

—1933

### Your Duty To-day

Believe in God
Lift yourself
Lift your family
Lift your clan
Lift your race
Lift your country
Lift your nation
        And be
An imperial whole.

—1933

### Your Duty To-morrow

WITH GOD'S GRACE—
Look back and help for humanity's sake.
Measure your charity by the acts of others toward you
    while you were climbing.

Forget not the past with all its good and ill reports.
Contemplate your future by the experiences you have had.
If you must strike to live, strike hard and sure.

—1933

## [Untitled]

If I were you, I would
Search myself
To find out if there is any
Good in me.

—1934

## Win The Fray!

1.  O! when the Negro makes himself a man,
        The wicked world will see a new parade;
    The blacks will march in one tremendous clan—
        A great phalanx of noble fighting braves.
2.  The day that Africa awakes, in deed,
        And black men cease to dream away the time,
    The scoffing tribes of other men will heed,
        The race's claims of sober righteousness.
3.  It's then for you to think and act to-day,
        And show of what good mettle you are made
    It's not what other men may do or say,
        But just how game you are to win the stake.

—1934

## A Recitative Song!

### (For Julius Winston Garvey.)

1. I am a little soldier, fighting hard for life,
   I came upon the scene of cruel human strife,
   My father taught me to be always good and true,
   And in the battle ever try to be a blue.
2. I've met so many hard and awful blows, you know,
   But friends, I heard that "we shall reap just what we sow,"
   So I shall e'er a Negro man of courage be,
   And work with other noble men who'll toil with me.
3. I promise to engage in what is good and right,
   And for the cause of race to make a manly fight;
   The world shall be my cautious battle stage,
   For I shall follow wisely footprints of old age.
4. The endless fight of men for right against the wrong,
   Shall steel my youthful courage on and make me strong;
   But I shall need God's help all seasons of the year,
   To safely fight for you with heart that's void of fear.
5. The Negro's cause is now beset with many darts,
   But we can win if we have true and loyal hearts;
   Young though I be, I'll stand and march with you,
   If you will serve and hold the line, like men—true blue.

—1934

## A Rallying Song

1. Oh glorious race of mighty men,
   The homeland calls to you;
   Our fathers wrought with faith divine,
   So let us march in line. (Refrain)

2.   If foe we meet across the way,
     Our courage hold on high,
     For Victory is near at hand,
     So march ye with the band.
     Refrain: Oh glorious race, Etc.

3.   Old Africa is calling you,
     So wave the banner high;
     No foe shall win the glorious day,
     Shout ye, and march and pray.
     Refrain: Oh glorious race, Etc.

4.   Our God is leading us away,
     And land and seas divide,
     For hosts are here in royal form,
     March on and fear no storm.
     Refrain: Oh glorious race, Etc.

5.   New Africa beholds the sight,
     The world will tremble then,
     Good men of might will worship God
     And bless the heaving sod.
     Refrain: Oh glorious race, Etc.

6.   Tell the people everywhere you go,
     "The day is here again,"
     The Ethiopian's God appears
     To deal with all affairs.

—1934

### Blackman!

What Is In Thy Bosom? Pluck It
    Out—Is It Genius, Is It Talent
For Something? Let's Have It.

—1934

## The Song Of The Negro Maid

I look at man in grim dismay;
He tried my virtue all to steal:
My heart is full of joy today,
No sin is on my soul I feel.

The guiling tongue of Adam's son,
Has left me free to see the light
The Master saw o'er Satan won,
In battles they did often fight.

The white man forced my head to bow,
My chastity to treat with scorn;
But I am queen of self, and now
I feel as pure as I was born.

With firm respect I love my race:
No one shall lead me thus astray,
Of kin to lose the ancient trace
That makes me what I am today.

—1934

## Find Yourself!

God made each man with something great—
The thing is to be found in you;
Please search and find the stuff remote,
And pine no more on awful fate.

The genius of mind is there,
It's hidden, yes, for each to find;
Dive down, my man, and find yourself,
And in the good of life do share.

The Negro has an equal chance
To make a world to suit himself;
Go then and work your mental plan,
Your life and fortune to enhance.

—1934

### Your Lesson!

1. The skies and stars are there, and sun and moon,
    They move and shine for you and me each day;
   Our journey here is short—exit is soon,
    In such a change to be I have no say.
2. But in the link between this life and death,
    I am the master of myself, I know;
   I gather knowledge with natural breath,
    And I shall surely reap just what I sow.
3. Yes, from the world I learn a lesson true,
    No race nor colour proves me less in clan;
   I need not quibble for or curse my hue,
    That makes of me, like anyone, a man.
4. My God, so great, has made all things and me,
    My place and grip on life are ever here;
   So inferior being I ne'er shall be,
    I learn from Nature grand, that's everywhere.

—1934

### Halt! America!

America of white men's rule,
    The God of Heaven calls to you;
You used the black man as a tool,
    And proved of faith and love untrue.

Your Christian faith is all a lie,
  If you do not some changes make;
You brought us here to make us die,
  But God will save us for His sake.

There is a call to make things right,
  And to your conscience we appeal:
For peace we are, we want no fight,
  We ask you but the wound to heal.

We've laboured long in many fields,
  To clear your waste and barren lands:
We fought your wars with manly shields,
  But you've cast us off your hands.

America will flourish great,
  If love and truth abide within;
And so we call upon the State,
  To free itself from deadly sin.

The Negro's cause is holy word,
  And God proclaims the mighty truth,
The angels speak with flaming sword,
  And it is so to man forsooth.

                              —1934


## Going Wrong

My God! the world is going wrong
Frail man has made a mess of things:
And now the Devil seems on top,
Confusing Presidents and Kings.

Oh come, good Lord, with grace divine,
And stem the tide of human sin,

For left alone we'll ruin make,
And close the gate to enter in.

There's hell on every hand today,
And man is raising cain all round:
There're curses, blasphemies, galore,
Stop them, O Lord, and check the bound.

The Devil smiles at his good work,
And men do dance with satisfaction:
But hell let loose is sin on sin:
Send Lord your benediction.

In solemn notes the Negro cries:
"We are getting hell on every side,"
Come, Lord, and clean the dens of men,
And make us with the good abide.

                                        —1934


### Get Up And Work

The Negro sits and pines all day:
    His opportunities slip away;
Get up and work your mind my lord,
And grasp the good the days afford.—

                                        —1934


### George S. Schuyler Again

George S. Schuyler is a joke;
His brain must be like sausage pork,
Or he must be a "nutty" ass
To bray at those he cannot pass:
The man, if man he is, is crude;

His very looks is mighty rude,
He feeds on what his masters say,
And acts like monkey all at play.

He writes his soppy stuff each week,
The stuff of journalistic freak:
No one should worry over him,
But pass him with a good "boof, bim,"
A Negro man he claims to be,
And that puts us up on a tree:
If he should look at his old face,
He'd see the libel of his race.

—1934

### "Fire In The Flint!"

Oh yes, there's fire in the heart of man—
A beast is he when'er it pleases him:
He frowns upon the members of his clan,
And oft the lives of hosts and friends bedim.

A child of God as he was made to be,
He changes soul and character to boot;
And now he hates and kills with license free,
And smiles at all, to rob, to cheat and loot.

Not only does he plunder men for gain,
But prejudices practice 'gainst the weak,
He thus inflicts upon them awful pain,
And forces them to hope, in groanings meek.

The whites are great offenders 'gainst the Blacks;
They steal, they rape, they kill and punish hard
The sons of Ham, and whip them on their backs:
In hope alone they trust their gracious Lord.

To call it mortal sin, is mild rebuke:
It's man's most wicked way of treating man:
To gain the ends, his laws and ways impute
That men are different beings, and not one clan.

The centuries of life have left no seed
Of goodly change toward the the helpless weak;
With all the pleas and woes, man fails to heed;
But leaves the bending poor God's grace to seek.

A life for life, is not with men all true;
The strong corrupts, destroys and murders all;
And white men lynch the ones of darker hue,
Who have not rights nor laws on which to call.

And should you doubt the story I do tell,
I ask of you, investigate the facts:
Go South and see the men who live in hell—
Who get the kicks with burdens on their backs.

The mob will make the human skull a ball,
And trample on the foetus of the child:
Oh! this, of crime, is fun, yes, very small!
The "Crackers" think this sport but passing mild.

The fire in the heart of man is hell;
It's flint that burns throughout the night and day;
Yet with such creatures we must always dwell,
And groan, and weep, and die, but have no say.

                                        —1934


## Our Day!

The Bread of life is gift of God to man,
The blood of Christ is solace grand:

To eat the food of Love Divine,
Brings hope that leads to glory's land.

The glorious Sacrament of Christ
Is tonic to the soul each day:
A ransom in the Blood of love,
Is gain for those who humbly pray.

As sons of Ham we eat the Bread,
And drink the Holy Christian Blood:
Our hope is in the Grace of God,
For sufferings thus understood.

Our day will come with showers true,
For God on evil things will frown:
Almighty love is all we claim,
Though man destroys and keeps us down.

−1934

## The Mighty Three!

Three ancient Negroes gathered at the old Cross Roads,
An African, West Indian and American;
They talked of separation days of slavery,
And pledged ne'er more divided be in world of bravery.

"The tricks of olden times are ended now," they said,
And they must show united front to one and all;
"No more will distance keep us down or ranks divide,"
"So help our God!" the three did swear and all decide.

A bloody slave of sire made in ignorance,
Is sure not binding now, as then, they all agreed:
To God above they looked, all three, in vision clear,
And made a vow to save the race and have no fear.

United stand the Negro man in deeds of love,
A common weal of race to urge, and then to gain;
No more the three shall be apart in actions great,
But, hand in hand, march on to glorious fate.

This is the way for you and me in conflicts drawn,
By men who dare our ranks divide with wanton rule:
Bless ye, be firm, be strong, and stand "you mighty three;"
Press on, and look to God, till you are wholly free.

$$-1934$$

## Black And White

I'm black not white, which is no crime;
To have all things makes one so great:
If blacks did have, all whites would crave
More black to be for all that time.
The whites have ALL, in regal state,
And blacks do think them more sublime
But whites would think the blacks so brave
If they had greater wealth all time.

$$-1934$$

## The World Is Hell

The World is Hell as man shows it;
The creatures are of steel;
To live is of superior wit,
To fail is thus to feel.

No smile is genuine my friend,
Its all a pleasing lie;
Be ever ready to defend
Or shape your mind to die.

$$-1934$$

### A Tribute (?) To Hitler And Mussolini

Old Europe is a camp of armed men,
Of creatures cold and blue;
They live to kill, and yet pretend
They're friends to me and you.

America no better off,
Is watching Asia, too,
And all, combined, are mad,
Because of love untrue.

The human fellowship in God
Is lost to Europe's blood,
For man is but an angry beast,
Who spoils, like Noah's flood.

The Light of all the world must come,
To save the human race,
For Europe is a den of wolves,
Unfit to see God's face.

$-$1935


### The Conquering Race

I heard a cry from underneath,
It was the death pang of a slave;
A white man's sword was from its sheath,
And he to all the world was brave.

He slew the blackman for his wealth,
Although the victim had no arms;
At home his friends all drink his health
For deeds of courage he performs.

This is the boasted pride of men
Who roam the world for selfish gain:

The earth shall be the Devil's den,
So long as evil spirits reign.

The Cinemas delight the crowd
In deeds of hellish human crime;
Of this the nations now are proud,
As bandits rove from clime to clime.

                                    —1935


### The White, Sinful Church

The Church of God on Earth to-day
Is scandal of the King;
It teaches men to sing and pray,
For golden wealth to bring.
It sanctifies the cause of war,
And winks at evil deeds;
It sends its "saints" and men, afar,
To preach the victor's creeds.
The Blacks and Weaker Sets of Men
Are robbed and killed galore;
The Church looks o'er Commandments
     ten,
As tyrants kill some more.
The lands that God gave men to dwell
Are taken by the sword
As preachers go, their creeds to sell,
To those who heed their word.
Almighty God looks down on Earth
To see the Church in sin,
And so we hope for Cleansing Birth,
To let the Master in.
And when the Gentle Jesus leads,

The Priests and Pastors, too,
Shall see the growth of harvest seeds
That blend with every hue.

                                        —1935


## Modern Men

The men you meet are liars of the time,
As high as they may seem to you:
A statesman's ways are all sublime,
But ne'er a word of his is true.
The preacher talks for form alone,
And does like sinners bound for Hell:
To all these tricks the world is prone,
Although the Beadle rings his bell.
Between the State and Christian Church,
The poor are kept in their "good" place,
And if they kick, they'll be in lurch
With judge who stares them in the face.
It's God alone to save us all,
For not in man can any trust:
All mortals treat the rest like ball
They kick on field to yonder dust.
Next when your prayers you do say,
Ask God to come Himself to you:
For just as night comes after day
All men will prove to be untrue.
It may sound harsh to tell this tale,
But every man can vouch for it,
For he has had his timely sale
Of cruel conscience, bit by bit.

                                        —1935

## A Black Man's Speech To A White Man In America

I'm not as educated, sir, as thee,
But God Almighty's sun I see,
And you may treat me very hard for this,
But I His Holy Hand shall kiss.
I have no nation, none as great as yours
That kills and grabs beyond the shores;
I have no selfish laws to keep men down
And then upon them ever frown.
You have the wealth of land and sea and
    sky,
You boast as if you'd never die:
How great you are, my mighty earthly
    king,
So great that I must tribute bring!
But, sir, one day you'll surely be in Hell,
And then a story I will tell;
As Dives asked for quenching water then,
So will you all from that hot pen.
Your gilded pride is much in this your
    day—
It's time for you to gather hay—
And so you feed upon my sorry life,
And rob me of my home and wife.
My lands you say are yours, and minerals,
    too,
How sweet it is, dear sir, to you!
You kick me down and lash me on my
    back,
And when I cry there's one more whack.
But one good day will surely come for me,
When God of men will speak to thee,

And then the awful thunder clap will tell,
How far down you will be in Hell.

                                        —1935


### A Black Man's Prayer

Send Thy peace to all this world,
Lord of nations and of man—
Where blood banners are unfurled,
In their wicked sinful den.
Sin may reign upon the throne,
In man's way of seeing right;
Thou art Lord in truth; alone
Thou canst set all sin to flight.
Black men crushed to earth each day
Raise a voice of pleading now:
Come good Lord we all do pray,
Make the tyrants humbly bow.
For since God is God alone,
And vile man is man for that,
And will not of self atone,
Treat him, Lord, as virus rat.
White is great upon the earth,
Greater than the King of Kings:
This is sin of human birth
That the white man daily sings.
Thou art made to be so white
That no black man has a claim:
Could'st this, God, Be ever right
That you made us ill of fame?
Thou art God in every way,
Caring not for black nor white;

Then, O Lord! look down this day,
Turn the white man to the right.

—1935

### Get Up And Do

You sit and quarrel all your life,
And blame the moving world at large:
You fail to enter in the strife,
To sail in fortune's happy barge.

Get up my man and do the "stuff"
That leads to blazing glory's fame:
Hold on, and be like good Macduff,
And damn the man who'd foil you' name.

—1935

### Mussolini—Scourge Of God!

The day of gloom is here, O Lord!
And brought by wicked man to earth;
The Mussolini murder sword
Has doomed the Saviour's Holy birth.
The Rome that claims the Tree of Love
Has blessed the murderer's awful deed;
What blasphemy of God, above,
To satisfy a Caesar's greed?
While sober men do seek the way
Of Love and Holy Brotherhood,
There comes another "Roman day"
To spoil and rob us of the good.
Afric's Christian children cry,
To save us Lord from Rome and sin;

Do lead us on, yea, not to die,
But with the Cross to make us win.
The Blacks of all the world do praise
The Prince of Peace, for love so dear;
As Simon did in bygone days,
So do for us, and be Thou near.
The bluff of Rome's new human Scourge
Has reached to Heaven's inner Gate;
We pray he will not cross the gorge
That shields our father's ancient State.

                                    —1935


### The Fascist Brute

The gath'ring storm of hell let loose
Is Mussolini's way of death:
But sober men will ask God's truce
Before they lose their fearful breath.
A war to-day will but inflame
A world of thinking, waiting men:
With white and black its just the same,
They, all, shall break from out the pen.
And Communism here and there,
In Europe's land, America, too,
Shall join the blood march everywhere,
And make the world a hell for you.
No horn shall stop the great melee,
When shots have cleared the Roman
        guns:
The mad shall shout: "O we are free,
And death to all the blasted Huns."
When changes come, the Fascist brute
Shall see his awful, foolish sin:

The blackshirts play upon the lute,
But vict'ries they shall never win.
So stop them now and save the world,
And let us march with reason on,
The flag of love to be unfurled
Among the tribes of hopeful man.

—1935

### The Great (?) White Man

Adam, Eve and all the rest of men
Threw away the chart of holy life,
And becoming Satan's cruel children,
Waste the world in ceaseless strife.
Europe's sons are foremost now in craft.
Man designs to crush the higher self:
With their politics and racial graft
They sail o'er the world in hunt of pelf.
Mussolini's creed of grab and take
Was at first the Roman's highest law;
But, right now all life is set to stake
If the brutal human stroke has flaw.
Day by day we see the white man's sin
Making all the world a living hell,
Not a place for good to enter in,
No, except through burning shot and
       shell.
When the God of all made thinking man,
Placing him on earth to dwell in love,
Angels hoped to see the human clan
Blessing God, the gracious King above.
Fight to kill, is watchword of the day:
White men have no other human urge:

They have ceased to worship God, to
   pray;
But they glory in the sinful surge.
Robbing all the lands beyond the sea,
Making slaves and cheating children, too,
White men claim that they are great and
   free,
Much more great than ravished me and
   you.

—1935

### The Beast Of Rome

Down from the Seven Hills of Rome
Came brutes in human form,
They left their cursèd, sinful home
Our Motherland to storm:
Yes, led by Mussolini's own son,
They passed the Old Canal,
And when their war was just begun
They fought like cannibal.

The Rome of sin and human hate
Has plagued the world before,
But God will serve their awful fate
On Ethiopia's shore.
Their guns and gas may threaten all
As hymns they sing at home.
But ere Adowa's final fall
The fight shall pass from Rome.

The God Who is above nation
Shall speak with thunder loud;
He shall redeem His creation,
And pass from out the cloud.

The people pray to Him on High
To save the black man's land,
And so His Word shall never die
For he will be at hand.

Let Rome then purge herself of sin,
And stop the sacrilege,
For Mussolini ne'er shall win
The black man's heritage.
The curse of all the world is pride,
That venal Rome assume,
With Mussolini, as beside
D'Annunzio at Fiume.

—1935

### Be King Of Circumstances

The rise of nations and of men
Record the struggles passed and won,
But none may tell just where and when
The urge did come and thus begun.
It might have been through glorious deeds
Performed by earlier men of fame,
Whose inspiration often leads
To visions that remake a name.

A Constantine, Alexander, too,
A Hannibal and Caesar great
May change the thought of even you
And give a hero to the State.
To read the deeds of men renowned
Will make you choose a given course
That often strikes the note profound,
Revealing thus the man of force.

The deeds we do must make the race
And force the nation to the top,
And when we gain the honour place
We forge ahead and never stop.
Keep winning more and still some more,
And set a pace for fainter heart;
Your deeds shall spread from shore to
    shore,
And worlds shall know you played your
    part.

Though black of race you are, my friend,
Your part in life is ever here:
There's work for you; the human trend
Calls for each one to have his share.
Go then and play your part to-day,
And think that you are king of all
Circumstances that come your way.
Before which you must never fall.

                                    —1935


### The Brutal Crime

The Beast of Rome sent forth his might
'Gainst Ethiopia's silent hosts,
And in battle went the men
Who haunt the hills and plains like ghosts.

Askaris, grinning soldiers,
Like April fools at summer play,
Did shoulder arms for Italy
To give the Beast of Rome the day.

When blacks fight blacks in white men's wars
They're fools for all their valiant pain,

For they shall never hope for right
In whatsoever is the gain.

Ras Gugsa, ignoble of fame,
Betrayed the Emperor's goodwill;
His head should be upon the block,
For Negroes then to curse at will.

When Mussolini challenged us,
He knew the weakness of the men;
To feed and pat them on the back
Was all, to get them in the pen.

The cursed fool who fell for Rome,
And marched against the Motherland,
Should never live to tell the tale
Of his unholy traitor-band.

The Psalmist sung of days to come,
And God himself did bless the time,
And yet the grinning fool of race
Betrays the cause that is sublime.

When all is o'er, and God prevails,
The curse of all the world shall be
Upon the heads of traitor-blacks
Who failed to make their country free.

—1935

### The Mystery

All life is mystery to man
Who speculates the cause,
His final clue is God alone
Who made and holds the laws.

From Africa to Ancient Greece
The light of knowledge flew,
But up to now the truths revealed
Go back to what man knew.

There is a God above all things
His wisdom is complete,
As ages come and ages go
To leave us at His feet.
Eternity will ever be
The gauge of finite man,
For life to him is just a song
In passing with the clan.

We come to live, then go again,
And still some more are we,
As Nature blends in every form
Beyond the land and sea.
We're ever looking on before
To see life's moving train,
And as we go we leave behind
The same old human pain.

—1935


### Those Who Know

You may not know, and that is all
That causes you to fail in life;
All men should know, and thus not fall
The victims of the heartless strife.
Know what? Know what is right and wrong,
Know just the things that daily count,
That go to make all life a song,
And cause the wise to climb the mount.

To make man know, is task, indeed,
For some are prone to waste all time:
It's only few who see the need
To probe and probe, then climb and climb,
The midnight light, the daily grind,
Are tasks that count for real success
In life of those not left behind,
Whom Nature chooses then to bless.

The failing men you meet each day,
Who curse their fate, and damn the rest,
Are just the sleeping ones who play
While others work to reach the best.
All life must be a useful plan,
That calls for daily, serious work—
The work that wrings the best from man—
The work that cowards often shirk.

All honour to the men who know,
By seeking after Nature's truths:
In wisdom they shall ever grow,
While others hum the awful "blues"
Go now and search for what there is—
The knowledge of the Universe—
Make it yours, as the other, his,
And be as good, but not the worse.

—1935


## The White Man—Spirit Of Mussolini

The white man stands with murd'rous gaze,
And looks with envy at all wealth;
For gold he has a burning craze
That crowns him with his bloody stealth.
From shore to shore he roams at large,

With maxim guns and poisoned darts:
He sails aboard his nimble barge
To rip and bleed his victims' hearts.

To India he goes with glee
For stores of shining, precious stones;
And off to China for his tea,
And Africa for ivory-bones.
The land he takes with gun in hand,
And chains the natives to the heel:
He often used the iron-brand
To mark the slaves that he would steal.

Through Egypt's land he beats the trail,
That leads to blooming cotton fields;
From ship to barge he goes on rail
That brings him on the natives' heels.
The Sudanese, in fields of white,
Must pick the cotton at his will;
Just he alone of all is right
When he at pleasure shoots to kill.

The Congo Basin had its crime,
Of hands chopped off by Leopold,
For rubber wealth, of franc and dime,
The blacks were murdered stiff and cold:
And Cecil Rhodes, in Kimberly,
Did flog the mining natives, too,
That ladies might, at "Wemberly,"
Wear diamonds with the shades of blue.

In Old America of slaves,
John Hawkins did his roaring trade,
For Indians were killed by braves
Who fought like Custus's Brigade.
The blacks were kept in clanking chain,

Two hundred years, and little more:
The Bishops spurned the hellish pain,
And blessed the trips from Afric's shore.

West Indian nights were like the day,
As slaves worked on and on to die.
For sugar and old rum did pay
Much more than barley and the rye.
Great fortunes there were made in sin,
By lords and gentlemen at large,
Whose homes you could not enter in,
Except you sailed in their good barge.

But this, O God, is known to you,
So time will bring your message down,
And then from out the azure blue
Shall come the Prince with heaven's crown.
That day shall see the white man gone,
To place in store for cruel man—
For saints of earth were really born
To rise above the murd'rous clan.

—1935


### The New Day

The Negro slept a thousand years,
    While white men moved along,
And so he sheds his bitter tears,
    As white men sing their song.

Another day has just begun,
    For white and black alike;
The white man greets it with his gun:
    Will Negroes ever strike?

—1936

### The Brute Of History

When years have passed to shaded memory,
　　And all reflect on things of yore,
The name o'Benito Mussolini
　　Shall haunt good men on every shore.

Like John, the Devil, to the saintly soul,
　　The Duce shall flash his fangs of flame,
And every child will find a hiding hole,
　　In fear of Roman with his name.

　　　　　　　　　　　　　　　　—1936


### Your Triumphs And Your Fears

Think not that all is lost to you,
　　Except you fail yourself in all:
The world will grant to you your due
　　In greatness and in your downfall.

In greatness you will have her smiles;
　　In your downfall you'll have your tears:
But on the way, the travelled miles
　　Will mark your triumphs and your fears.

Up Negro! To the mountain top!
　　Up to the peak of all that's good!
Rest not in sorrow's wasteful lap,
　　But reach the heights where gods once
　　　　stood.

　　　　　　　　　　　　　　　　—1936


### Hell's Back Door

The way we flitter through our span,
　　And break the laws of loveliness,

Does show an open Hell for man
  On earth, with all his naughtiness.
The coming and the going out,
  Are just the same, in sinfulness;
Of all our ways, there is no doubt,
  For they do show our wretchedness.
We've made a back door right to Hell,
  And we do slip ourselves within:
From Adam down, the records tell
  That man is full of mortal sin.
To close completely Hell's back door,
  We have to turn our faces round,
And this should be for rich and poor,
  If man's best virtues must be found.
We'll have to change the Hero's mark,
  And set examples good, in deed:
No Alexander's deeds, most dark,
  Nor Caesar's crimes should be our creed;
Napoleons should be tabooed,
  And cruel Mussolinis, too:
The deeds of Jesus should be wooed,
  To make of life a course more true.
To glorify the beast in man,
  And set it up in marble, tall,
Is way to crucify each one,
  Who under tyrants often fall.
When we do cease to honour sin,
  And praise but that of Christian love,
We'll find a world worth living in,
  As pattern of the realm above.
Yes, let us close our Hell's back door,
  And burn the reptiles of the race,
Not flesh, but records praised before,
  But now to man a foul disgrace.

In this your Mussolini's doom,
  No one will try to be as he;
But seek to rest in peace, in tomb
  That marks the love of liberty.

—1936

### The Smell Of Mussolini

When summer days have gayly passed away,
  And winter months have darkly come again,
And when sweet spring does bring the laughing
    day,
  There still shall be a bloody, ling'ring stain;
It's name and character of Mussolini,
  The brute who killed with bombs of liquid
    flame;
We hate him, yes we hate him, good and plenty;
  We hate the "smell" of that most brutal
    name.
A Roman steeped in envy and murder,
  He stole the lands of all the Christian blacks;
But he shall have his gaseous thunder
  Thrown back some day on mad Italians' backs;
And when that day does really come, my men,
  We will give it to them with bolts of steel,
And run the Italian out his bloody den.
  To make him see the Negro's commonweal.
A thousand years may be the waiting time,
  To strike the brute that came from cursed
    Rome;
But keep your courage high and quite sublime,
  For that great day to hit the trail for home;
For every Roman soldier shall fall down,

And lick the dust in very penitence,
As Hannibal did make them kiss the ground,
   We too shall crush them in our self defence.
No one shall help an Italian man,
   In any way of other human beings,
For he is one with Mussolini's clan
   That seek to change the world to Roman
      scenes:
Let all Italians live and die in shame,
   For what their Mad Dog did to our dear home:
Their Mussolini's bloody, savage name
   Smells stink from Addis back to sinful Rome.
No cause that links Italian liberty
   Shall have appeal to us, in peace or war;
No one will ask us in our sobriety
   To help the Italian, near or far:
In clash of arms, on Europe's fields of blood,
   No help must Negroes give to Roman cause,
For it must be for ever understood
   That Italians keep no sacred laws.
We shall march past the ancient Vatican,
   To sack the gates of Italian Rome,
And make them feel the hand of vengeful man,
   Who first was driven from his natural home:
With English, German, French or other hordes,
   We'll march to crush the Italian dog,
And at the points of gleaming, shining swords,
   We'll lay quite low the violent, Roman hog.

                                                          –1936


### Il Duce—The Brute

Tell all the world about the crime,
   Of Roman might against the right:

Oh tell it now, in every clime,
　　The deeds as dark as darkest night:
From Hell the thought of conquest came
　　To Italy's most crafty son,
Duce Mussolini is his name,
　　And he a Devil's crown has won.
With all the elements of God
　　Intended for man's blessed use,
He tore men's flesh and soaked the sod
　　With blood—thus gifts of God abuse.
A man of savage Roman tribe,
　　Il Duce has done his brutal worse;
To him will Roman fate ascribe
　　The curse that comes in even course.
Tell Abyssinians now to rise
　　Against Italians' mailed fists,
And never sleep till each man dies,
　　If he our freedom still resists.

—1936

## Get Up And Go!

Please clear the way and let me pass,
　　If you intend to give up here:
It seems a shame that you should yield
　　Your life without its fullest share.

You are a coward for your pains,
　　To come this way, and then blow out:
Real men are made of stuff to last,
　　Which they, themselves, would never doubt.

Get up! You broken bits of flesh!
　　Take courage and go fighting on;

For every black man there's a day,
    Which pride in race has well begun.

—1936

### The Devil In Mussolini

When God did make the world and all
He laid a righteous plan of things:
He never meant to harbour sin
Among mankind with all their kings.
He did establish holy law
To rule the mighty universe,
And everything that He did make
Was bound to follow such a course.
But evil crept into man's life,
And wasted all that Goodness gave,
And strife was stirred between the two
That pressed man into his sad grave:
The Devil and the Lord of Host
Have fought upon the plains of life,
And still we see the conflicts rage
With God on top in every strife.
The Caesars came and went their way,
With Alexander and his kind,
Napoleon did also come
With Mussolini close behind;
The latter devil raised his sword
To bleed a world of peaceful men.
And Roman sin proclaimed him great
For his descent on God's children.
This devil in mad human form,
Performs his tricks and deeds with boast:
He prates on Italy's great fame
And challenges the Lord of Host,

The fight goes on between the two,
To end as did the rest before,
For God must win in every cause
That man threatens on any shore.
The time will come when every hand
Will smite the Mad Dog on the head,
And he will pass away to Hell
And leave his stain among the dead.
This Mussolini—devil-man—
Has come from out the darkest cave,
And savage-like, in looks and deeds,
He seeks to take the life God gave.
No soul can this vile madman give,
No creature can he ever make,
Yet he would bleed all men to death
And all for vanity's sole sake.
He leads the march 'gainst black and white,
To crown himself the lord of earth,
But whilst he gains, for just a while,
His triumphs are just devil's mirth.
The time will come to chain his feet
And hands, like all the devil's gone,
And he will be just one more fool
Who from satanic womb was born.
Pray down the Devil of the hills—
The hills of Roman wickedness,
And look to God, the King of Peace,
Who reigns for human blessedness.

—1936


### Far Up The Heights

Who said the Black Man never lived
    In History with his deeds most great?

The liar, thief and cowardly man
    Who tries to boss the Negro's fate.

He gave to Europe codes of laws,
    And took the Greeks from out their
        pen:
He sent his gods to foreign lands
    To show the light to other men.

Let Black Men feel as proud men should,
    For they do have a past most bright:
They gave out thoughts and made men
        think
Of them as gods far up the height.—

                           —1937


## Revenge

Not yesterday, but centuries long,
The Romans hated all of Negro blood,
For Hannibal did slay the crew,
As Carthage marched to martial song.
Again Adowa made them halt,
When Menelik did crush them low:
He proved the Blacks were timely men—
The heroes still without a fault.

But Italy kept crying out,
And longed for day of victory:
With Mussolini, courage came,
To fight to win without a doubt:
They used the weapons not allowed,
And took advantage as they went:
They crushed Selassie's mighty host
With Blacks Badoglio followed.

The Blacks shall come together now,
And they shall blast the way again:
Revenge is sweet! the Romans say;
Revenge! is on the Black Man's brow.
O sing the song of Carthage, great,
O sing the song of Afric', free:
The day will come to win again,
And pass to Italy her fate.

No man shall stop the moving throng
That goes to snatch the victory:
The world has bled the Black Man's heart,
And downed him, too, with all the wrong.
Come now and go in vision clear,
Right up to good Adowa's mount,
And let Italians ever feel
The dash of weapons in their rear.

If not on Ethiopian land,
Go, follow them where'er they go:
Join English, French or Russian, too,
And all together strike the band—
That band of Roman renegades—
Blood-thirsty men of Fascist's creed;
With Mussolini as their head
They'll die by gas and hot grenades.

Revenge is all! it's written there,
And Blacks will ne'er forget the call:
Like gods of old, let's live on high,
And each one dream of glory, fair.
The Rome of sin shall fall again,
As Addis rise toward the sun;
So pledge your word to sacred trust
And hurl Italians to the plain.

—1937

### Ras Nasibu Of Ogaden

A king has fallen on the field—
The field of war, but not by shot,
Nor even through a broken shield:
He died in exile—awful lot!
Ras Nasibu of Ogaden
Is he—the greatest of his tribe—
The man who led his valiant men
With Wehib Pasha at his side.

He died in Switzerland—afar,
Of broken heart in his exile:
He saw the end of that sad war
In which he fought without a smile.
The Brute of Italy had sent
His liquid flames of steady death
And tanks that ploughed and also rent
The land and stole the hero's breath.

This Mussolini, vile of heart,
Who plagues the world with devil tricks,
Has caused a king to lose his part
In building glory with his bricks.
The dream of Abyssinia, great,
Was dear to Nasibu's own heart;
But he has met an awful fate,
And failed in this to do his part.

The Negroes of the world shall wait
To take their stand against the foe,
And when they fight to win their State
They'll make Italians drink their woe.
A Fascist king shall never rule
The Blacks of all the lands we know:
The Negro shall be no foot-stool,
But give to all the seeds they sow.

Let's honour Nasibu's fair name,
And damn the Mussolini tribe:
This Abyssinian's splendid fame
Shall live through pen of Negro scribe.
Look out for time, that's coming soon,
To strike Italian Fascists down:
To us 'twill be a glorious boon
To have them sprawling on the ground.

−1937

### The Fall Of Slavery
(For the Benefit of Haile Selassie and Benito Mussolini.)

The man who holds a slave and laughs at ease
    Is devil with a heart of hardest stone:
The man who also lives with pride to tease
    Humanity should oft be left alone.
All men should have the freedom of all rights,
    For nature made no sovereign but the soul,
And all should look toward the glorious heights,
    To seek the sweet enjoyment of the whole.

When selfish creature, void of love for man,
    Inflicts his will upon the helpless weak,
All else should spurn him, as they can,
    To force him from the sovereign evil peak.
The thoughtful man who loves his brothers well,
    Is king to keep upon an earthly throne;
But slavers all should go right down to Hell,
    To sleep upon the slabs of burning stone.

The precious life of man demands a will
    To fight to hold the trust of his defence,
Though tyrants would all manly freedom kill,

True knights of love should guard the human
    fence.
Let's set the human standard high for all,
    And see that pompous kings and lords obey,
And when they fail through sin, proclaim their fall,
    And hasten in for all the freedman's day.

                                   −1937

### Ras Desta

The flow'r of a nation's strength
Had thrown their valour and their might
Against the charging hordes of death
In history's most unequal fight!
One man remained—the last of them—
To stand for Ethiopia:
All else surrendered, died or fled
But, he, the lion-hearted—Ras Desta.

Graziani, Italian butcher
Had valiant Desta quickly shot,
To seal his lips and tie his hands
In fear of what he called a plot.
With death of such a noble man,
A reign has passed to history;
But time will bring to us again
More men to fight for victory.

                                   −1937

### Wanting To Desert

A Negro who got rich did stray
    To claim he was not of the race,

But all the world could only say
　　He was a fool and sore disgrace.

You cannot change your skin, my man,
　　For Nature made you as you are;
Your wish to break your father's clan
　　Is ignorance that goes too far.

The woman of another race
　　You choose to share your fortune with
And have her take your mother's place
　　May slay you as in Siren's myth.

And when you find the deed unwise
　　It will be late, too late to mend,
For then the race you did despise
　　Will count you out with traitor's end.

　　　　　　　　　　　　　　−1937


### Broken Hearts

Broken hearts are flung to Hell's outpost,
Death and desolation tease the land;
This is due to Fascists' wildest boast
That has plagued mankind on every hand.
Down with Mussolini's creed of greed;
Down with all his forms of Roman pride;
Up with love and charity, in deed,
And with all that's true and should abide.
War is threatened everywhere we turn;
People's hearts are sad in mad despair,
Millions work on steel with hands that burn
All to cause the deadly things we fear.
Kill and kill, and still go killing more,
Is the order of the Fascist crew;

Kill them all on every foreign shore,
Kill them now, and not a paltry few.
Now we have the crew of men of might,
Blessed by Church and Holy (?) Roman state;
All they want are men to always fight,
Just to make their class forever great.
Stop the crew that seeks to wreck all life;
Stop the mad dogs at their Roman Game;
They who love the blood of human strife
Must be stopped in God Almighty's name.

—1937

### My Trip To The West Indies

My trip to West Indies has proved a boon;
I hope to make the trip again quite soon.
I met there men and women, children, too,
Whose hearts rang out with joys and grace
    quite true.
I ne'er shall joys of such a kind forget,
As coming from those friends out there I met.

—1937

### What We See

To look into the world of sin,
And see men shine like burning gold,
To ask myself from right within,
Can I be just the same—as bold?
And out the answer comes to me:
"The same that governs them, does you."

Its just the way you look, you see—
But of all things, be good and true.

                                    —1937


### The Rise Of The Negro

To rise and demonstrate en masse
Is way to make the oppressor think,
And so the Negro in his Class,
Sends forth his message to the King.

The King, a symbol of the State,
Sends forth his men to find what's wrong,
And back comes word of awful fate
On which the lives of men do hang.

The State assumes its task at last,
And makes an effort to amend
The wrongs that reigned throughout the past
By giving heed, though laws defend.

                                    —1938


### Man's Ambition

I dig my grave and lie in it,
And as I dig, I show to men
The tombstone that shall o'er me sit,
As I repose within my den.

[A] common grave be then my lot,
My deeds were of no lasting good,
And I shall lie and only rot,
Remembered not by neighbourhood.

                                    —1938

### To Think As Man

Round and round the Negro goes,
    Looking for a place of rest,
Nowhere can he find the place,
    Till he joins the army West.

This is due to lack of mind,
    Mind, without a will that counts;
Let the Negro think as man,
    Then for him there is no doubts.

—1939

# 6

## From *Universal Negro Improvement Association Convention Hymns* (1934)

## The Fight Is On

1. The fight is on to-day,
      The glory is at hand;
   No more must we delay,
      But join the marching band.

Chorus:

      The field is ever open,
         For those of courage great,
      For Heav'n has sent its token,
         So march to glorious fate.

2. The Prophets told us when
      The time would come to speak,
   And through the greatest men
      God's help, in faith, to seek.

3. Throughout the live long day,
      As battles we do fight,
   The Cross of Christ display,
      To keep Him all in sight.

4. In conflicts of the night,
      The stars will lead us on,
   So strike with all your might,
      And raise the Pilgrim's song.

## Afric's Love

1. When Afric's sun was setting fast
      The Prophets told the tale,
   But Psalmists said she'd win at last
      And pass beyond the vale.

Chorus:

> Come sing the song of Afric's love
>> The love of God so dear,
> The Father great in realms above,
>> The greatest when so near.

2. The day has come for us to see
>> The glory of our name,
> The hour of our jubilee
>> Will crown our greatest fame.

3. The hand of God is showing how
>> Our princes shall arrive;
> Old Egypt's land is throbbing now
>> With souls that are alive.

4. For ages past our sons were slain
>> On altars far and near,
> But all was destined, purging pain
>> To point the way so fair.

5. As Israel's people suffered long,
>> So Afric's host must do,
> But ours shall be the joyous song
>> By hearts most firm and true.

6. When tides of ocean cease to be,
>> Our joys will be immense,
> For that will be our jubilee
>> Our faith this day commence.

### Life's Procession

When time shall cease, in moving hour,
And Nature's laws revert to plan,
The beasts and insects, with the flower,
Shall pass in order with vile man.

The sinners will, in grouping file,
In human Autumn's ordered spell,
Go speeding on in mournful style,
Right to the flooded gates of Hell.

With wonder and amazement then,
The rich will look upon the poor;
But none shall be the same old men
Who often closed the Saviour's door.

By sins and virtues firm, each one
Shall have his rightful final pay;
No other choice will be for man
On this the final Judgment Day.

No wealth, no pull nor influence
Will save the cruel human crust;
With sin, each one will go from thence
To punishment of venal dust.

The virtues of the Mundane Life
Shall lead the subjects to The Crown,
But those of sin shall see the strife,
When Angels strike the culprits down.


### Freedom's Noble Cause
### 1834-1934

1.  Behold the day, a cent'ry old,
        When fathers' cares were lifted off:
    No more, as chattels to be sold,
        On block on farm, on ship or wharf.

2.  The sins of other men had made
        The world a living hell those days;
    But even as all sin do fade,
        The curse is gone, true freedom says.

3.    Profound regret we manifest
          That slavery brought us here:
      But God has done for us the best,
          And kept us in His kindly care.

4.    And now we rise as children new,
          To fight the battles fresh and keen:
      Our people, then, were sad and few,
          But now the millions can be seen.

5.    Good Buxton fought for us the fight
          With Knibbs, Wilberforce, Clarkson, too:
      They saw the awful, dreary night
          That shadowed us, of darkest hue.

6.    The hearts of England, called they out,
          Good Christian men, as they did prove:
      No stone unturned was left about,
          To ease us from the hellish grove.

7.    A century of histories
          Has brought us salving, trusting laws;
      And so we bless their memories,
          And sing for freedom's noble cause.


## A National Hymn

1.    Oh God of ages past, and age that ne'er shall end
          Bless Thou our fervent hope,
      And to our President Thy graces lend
          And bless our fervent hope.

Refrain:
          Bless Thou our fervent hope
              And lead us always right,
          Bless Thou our fervent hope
              In battles we may fight.

2.    Give him superb the power to defeat the foe
          And lead him always right,
      Let us not drink the draught of human woe
          But lead us always right.

3.    Frustrate the enemies and make us sure to win,
          In battles we may fight,
      Against the world and wicked men of sin
          For battles we may fight.

4.    Triumphant ever make us be in holy war,
          Our enemies to crush:
      From earth and distant planes and realms afar
          All foes we hope to crush.


### Jubilee

1.    Jubilee has come to-day,
          Praise to God the only King;
      Centuries have passed away,
          And good freedom's rights begin.

2.    Chains and blocks are gone to hell,
          Souls of men and women too;
      Saintly Prophets did all tell
          Slavers, hardy, story true.

3.    Come what may I'm free to dwell
          Where the sun and stars do shine;
      Never more can slavers sell
          This triumphant soul of mine.

4.    When from regions far away,
          Creatures black of skin were brought,
      Worldly men were glad to pay
          Prices great for those they bought.

5.      Better men of noble blood
            Fought the tyrants all the way;
        They before the world had stood,
            Fighting for good freedom's day.

6.      Now the day has come with joy,
            Hearts are glad throughout the land;
        Praises loud we now employ,
            Blessing those of Buxton's band.


### Centenary's Day

1.      A hundred years have passed and gone,
            And we are toiling still abroad;
        But we are not dismayed, forlorn,
            Nor hopeless of redeeming God.

2.      Our fathers bore the stinging lash
            Of centuries of slavery's crime;
        But we are here without abash,
            For we shall win in God's good time.

3.      We wish no evil, harm or hurt,
            To those who kept us down so long;
        We join with them in ways alert,
            To guard good freedom's happy song.

4.      To Afric's shore we're bound again,
            In freedom's glory won at large;
        In thoughts we claim a just bargain,
            To sail in liberty's fair barge.

5.      The world is conscious now of wrongs
            To us the sufferers had done;
        But now to each, who claims, belongs
            The truth—the light of God's own Son.

6.    We wish to live in peace alone,
    And bless all men for goodness' sake:
We praise the Lord on Glory's throne;
    To Him our Altars we do make.

## A Rallying Song

1.    Oh glorious race of mighty men,
    The homeland calls to you;
    Our fathers wrought with faith divine,
    So let us march in line. (Refrain)

2.    If foe we meet across the way,
    Our courage hold on high,
    For Victory is near at hand,
    So march ye with the band.
    Refrain: Oh glorious race, Etc

3.    Old Africa is calling you,
    So wave the banner high;
    No foe shall win the glorious day,
    Shout ye, and march and pray.
    Refrain: Oh glorious race, Etc.

4.    Our God is leading us away,
    And land and seas divide,
    For hosts are here in royal form,
    March on and fear no storm.
    Refrain: Oh glorious race, Etc.

5.    New Africa beholds the sight,
    The world will tremble then,
    Good men of might will worship God
    And bless the heaving sod.
    Refrain: Oh glorious race, Etc.

6.     Tell the people everywhere you go,
       "The day is here again,"
       The Ethiopian's God appears
       To deal with all affairs.


### Glory To The Lord

1.     Glory to Thy ways O Lord!
           We praise Thy Holy Name:
       Sacred is the precious word
           That tells the Christian's claim.

2.     Children of the Blood of Love,
           We bow before Thy Throne;
       Faith in Thee, the Hope above,
           Shall be our corner-stone.

3.     Bethel's star is guide to Thee,
           For Angels point the way:
       We at last are once more free
           To watch and sing and pray.

4.     Princes then shall come to rule,
           As Sheba did of old:
       Nevermore, as black foot-stool,
           Shall Afric's sons be sold.

5.     For ages we've been in pain,
           While trusting in the Psalms—
       Holy words of Saints so plain,
           Have come to us as balms.

6.     Lead us then O Prince of men!
           Against the mighty foes;
       Clear the world's most sinful den,
           And free us of our woes.

7.    When the day comes to an end,
        And we have won the fight,
      Faith and praises all shall blend,
        In welcome of the night.


### For He Is God

The Eternal hills are green in tropic lands,
And snowy white in temperate zones;
At seasons of the year, when nature speaks,
Most changes come, as ocean sands:

The planets and their suns betray a force
That rules o'er mighty changing time—
That time that had no beginning of day—
The time that runs its fullest course.

Almighty God is Master over all—
The crowning hills and valleys, too;
The oceans move at His eternal will,
And thus the terrestrial ball,
When nature changes from her mood to mood
And sparrows fall, and men do die,
It's God alone who knows the mystery art—
The art of life, the living food.

No man can die, no hill can ever move,
Nor seasons come and flying go,
Without the knowledge of the Mighty Lord,
Who holds the Universe in grove;
The finite mind of men must always know
That God Supreme is really King:
True wisdom we should everlasting seek,
And in His Grace do daily grow,

        For He is God, and God is God,
        And no more gods shall e'er be God.

### The Hymn Of Glory

1.  We sing to Him triumphant,
        The God who reigns o'er men,
    We tell of crimes defiant,
        Against commandments ten.

2.  Our race's travail of the night,
        Has left us struggling on,
    In God Almighty's twilight,
        Another hope is born.

3.  All men have kicked and slain us,
        Across the narrow way,
    From Egypt to Damascus,
        Each one has had his day.

4.  But now the tide is turning,
        Confusions of the world,
    And Christ our Lord is coming,
        Our banners to unfurl.

5.  As Egypt gave Him freedom,
        By Angel's bidding, once,
    We hope to gain the Kingdom,
        While angels sing and dance.

6.  We chant the hymn of glory,
        And look to God above,
    Our heads, though dark and hoary,
        Shall claim the Saviour's love.

# Bibliographical Note

"The Tragedy of White Injustice" was published in a pamphlet of the same name by Amy Jacques Garvey (New York: 1927). The shorter poems, "Hail! United States of Africa!" and "Africa for the Africans," completed the work which carried an advertisement for Garvey's "Keep Cool." The pamphlet went through two further printings. "The Tragedy of White Injustice" also appeared twice in 1927 in the *Negro World*, weekly organ of Garvey's Universal Negro Improvement Association. Here it bore the title, "The White Man's Game; His Vanity Fair: With Apology to All Honest Friends."

The poems comprising *Selections From the Poetic Meditations of Marcus Garvey* were written, like all the others of 1927, while Garvey was incarcerated in Atlanta penitentiary. Amy Jacques Garvey collected and published them in pamphlet form (New York: 1927). Some of them also appeared in the *Negro World*, during 1927.

The song, "Keep Cool," with words by Garvey and music by Alexander Seymour, was described in the advertisement mentioned above as the "Song Hit of the Season." It was said to have been proclaimed a success by *The Music Trade News*. It was published in 1927 by Seymour Music Publishing Company of New York.

The three items "From the *Negro World*" appeared in that paper in 1927. Similarly, those "From the *Black Man*" appeared in Garvey's monthly magazine which began publication in Jamaica and later moved, with Garvey, to London.

The *Universal Negro Improvement Association Convention Hymns* (Kingston, Jamaica: 1934), is an almost entirely unknown work of Garvey. It contained, in addition to Garvey's own poems, some traditional Christian hymns as well as a few works of the UNIA's former musical director, Arnold J. Ford.